PUBLISHER NOTES

Cataloging-in-Publication Data has been applied for and may be obtained from the Library of Congress.

ISBN: 978-1-947215-04-7

Book design by Joseph Stevenson
Cover design by Joseph Stevenson

Printed and bound in U.S.A.

An imprint of Golden Valley Press, LLC

Golden Valley Press books are available at special discounts when purchased in quantity for premiums and promotions as well as fundraising or educational use. Special editions can also be created to specification. For details contact me@josephstevenson.com or the address below:

Golden Valley Press
PO BOX 531412
Henderson, NV 89052
www.josephstevenson.com

for Joshua

INTRODUCTION
HOW TO DRAW ANIMALS

Welcome to "Drawing with Joseph Stevenson", "How to draw Animals!" In this book you will learn the basics of drawing animals realistically.

As we go through the book, the techniques I use will be the same for all of the animals. I will have about 20 different animal examples and tutorials and my hope is that when you are finished you will be able to draw any animal you choose using the same techniques.

The process I have created and follow when drawing is a 6 step process. For each animal I will just have the steps drawn out in the same order each time. I will explain each step now so you can refer back if you get confused.

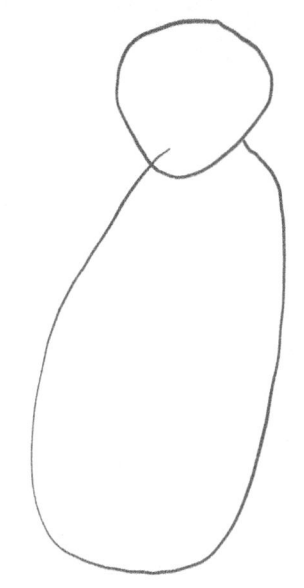

❶ The first step is drawing shapes. All drawings start with shapes. Sometimes they are shapes you are used to and other times you have to make some small adjustments. For our example we will draw a cat. I am going to start with two shapes, A circle for the head and an oval for the body.

I overlap the two shapes just a little and draw lightly with a pencil since these shapes are going to be erased later. Until you get to the last 2 -3 steps you will want to make sure and draw very lightly. The first 3 steps at least will get erased as you work your way through the process.

Now that you have your two shapes lightly drawn we will move to step two, which is adding in more detail.

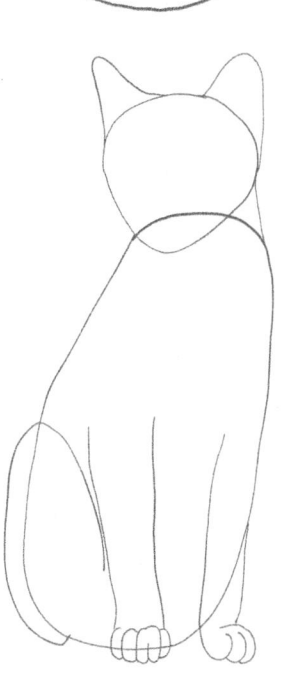

❷ You may notice our shapes just turned into the outline of a cat. If you are feeling worried about the detail, just take it one part at a time. First start with the head of the cat. There are two ears on the top. You can draw them any way you want but I add hoopes at the top of the circle.

Then the legs I do next. The legs them selves line up with each side of the head up and down. There is a gap between the legs about the distance of if we had a third leg in there. I add little hoopes on the bottoms for the paws.

Last I ad another oval to the left of the left leg. This is going to be the hind leg of the cat. I add a small line from the head to the shoulder as well.

3 Now for the third step we are going to get our cat's dimensions and shapes accurate in preparation for the detail portion of drawing. I hope you can still see the shapes we started with. Notice I have erased most of them away so we can see details of the cat more.

Erase where the ears, hind legs and head/shoulders meet. At this point it is helpful to remove those excess lines to focus on the next ones.

I also added in a tail that attaches to the hind leg and curves in under the front leg. I also added another paw to the left of the left leg. The left leg as well got extended up a little more to the shoulder.

The face is the biggest change. I added two eyes directly in the center. Between the two eyes and lower I added a small nose and mouth.

4 With the fourth step a lot doesn't change. From here we add another circle in each eye which will be the cat's pupil. The only other change I add at this point are lines inside the ears and around the body.

Although this doesn't seem like a big change it is actually very important. This cat has a lot of fur like many animals and we have to decide what direction we want the fur to go. Having these lines early on will help us to make certain areas of the cat dark and certain areas light.

I draw lines wherever I plan to have darker fur on the cat so I can keep track of my drawing and design. It also makes it easier to make sure your proportions are correct.

5 Now is what I consider to be the most fun part of drawing, the details. Using a pen I do strokes back and forth to create detail on the cat. Everywhere I added light lines on the cat will get a group of strokes from my pen.

I also add strokes anywhere I want there to be a shadow on my cat. This will make him more 3-dimensional. The back of the cat gets more strokes and the legs so that my cat looks a little more rounded.

I've added a few on his forehead as well. You may notice I have added dark pen inside the eyes with just a small white spot for light. I put a bit of speckles for his wiskers too and a little dark above the eyes. You may want to call it good at this point but I prefer to keep going and add lighter strokes to my cat.

❻   The last part of all my drawings and my cat is the final detail strokes. I have zoomed in to make it easier to see. I use pencil for these strokes instead of pen like before. You'll notice I use the same technique but I add lines back and forth in-between the dark ones to fill in my cat more. I also leave my cat's chest white so it has more dimension.

All of my animals are drawn the same way. As long as you get the shapes right in the first few steps, the shading and strokes can go any way you choose and still look good.

On my cat I could have put the stripes anywhere I wanted. I could have had his paw up in the air instead of on the ground. Maybe next time I will have him looking to the right or maybe we will only be able to see his back.

Once you learn the basics of shapes and shading you should be able to draw any animal you choose.

FINAL NOTE: Drawing is a talent. It is a talent that can be developed but a talent none-the-less. It will take time to get good at drawing. For some people it will take longer than others, but the key is to not get discouraged if you feel like it is taking a while. I have been drawing for as long as I can remember. Drawing this cat took me about 15 minutes.

It might take you 2 hours or 10 minutes. The point I'm trying to make is don't get discouraged and keep at it!

Once you get the hang of it drawing is a blast!

Have fun and good luck!

- Joseph
    Stevenson

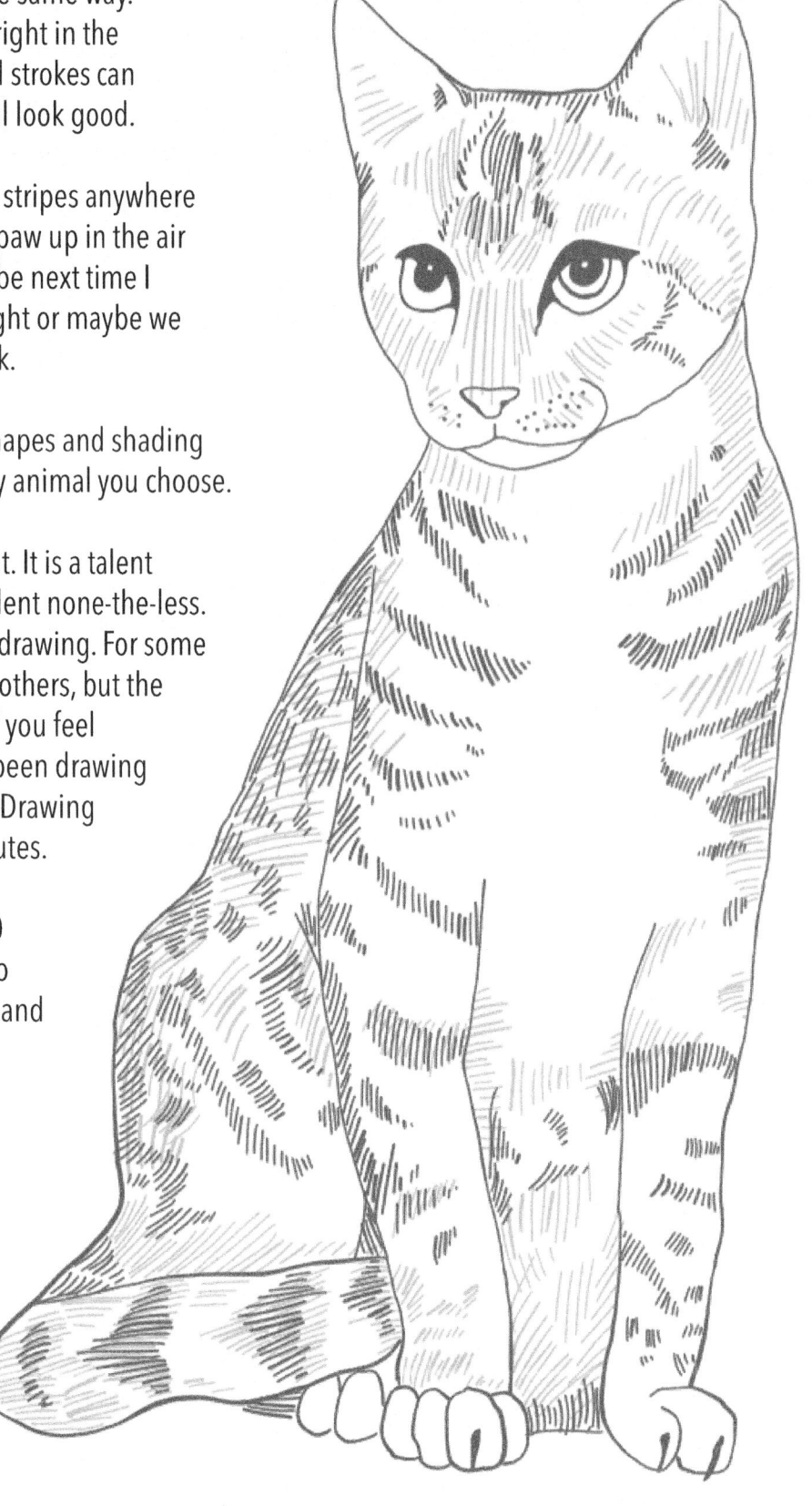

DRAWING A DOG

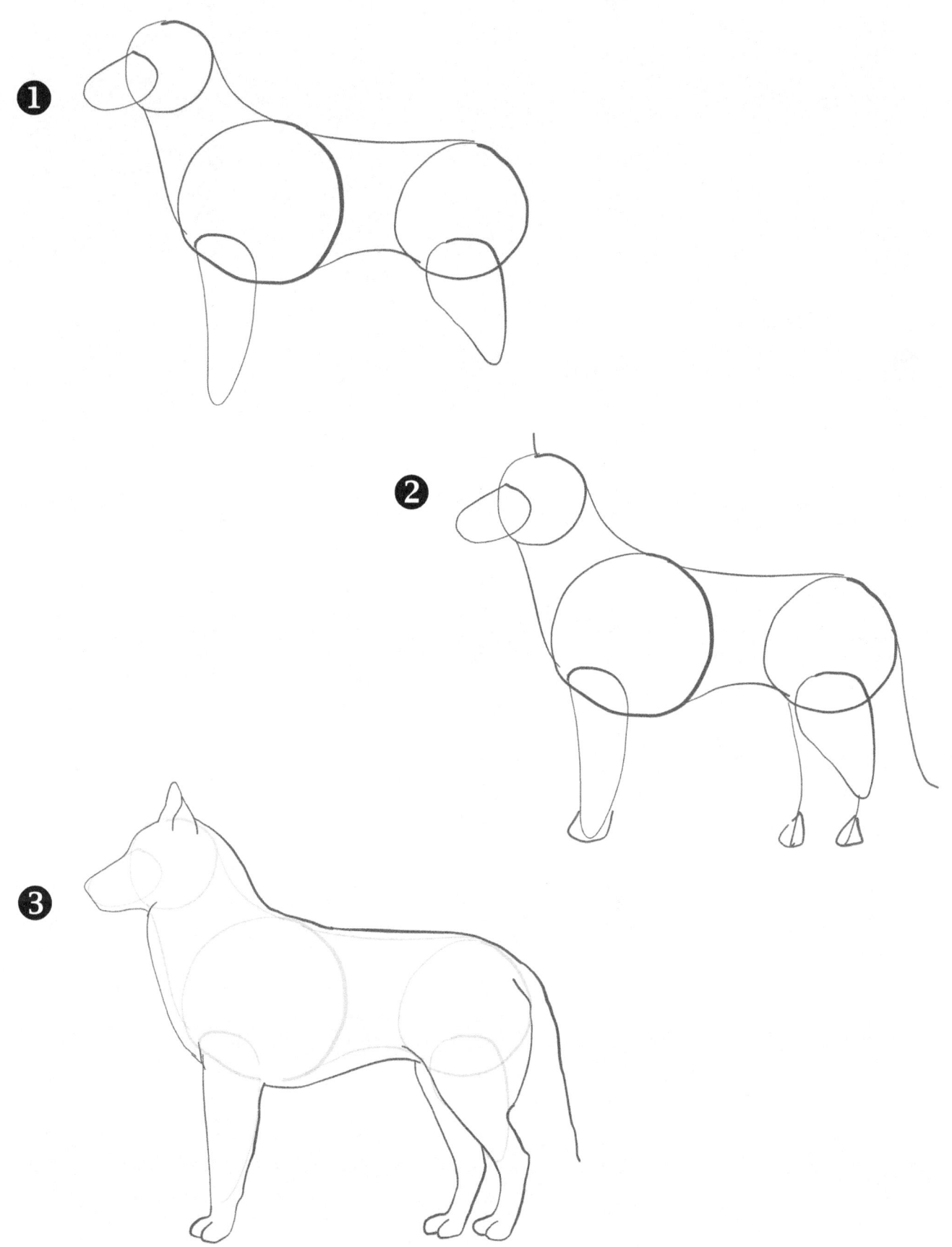

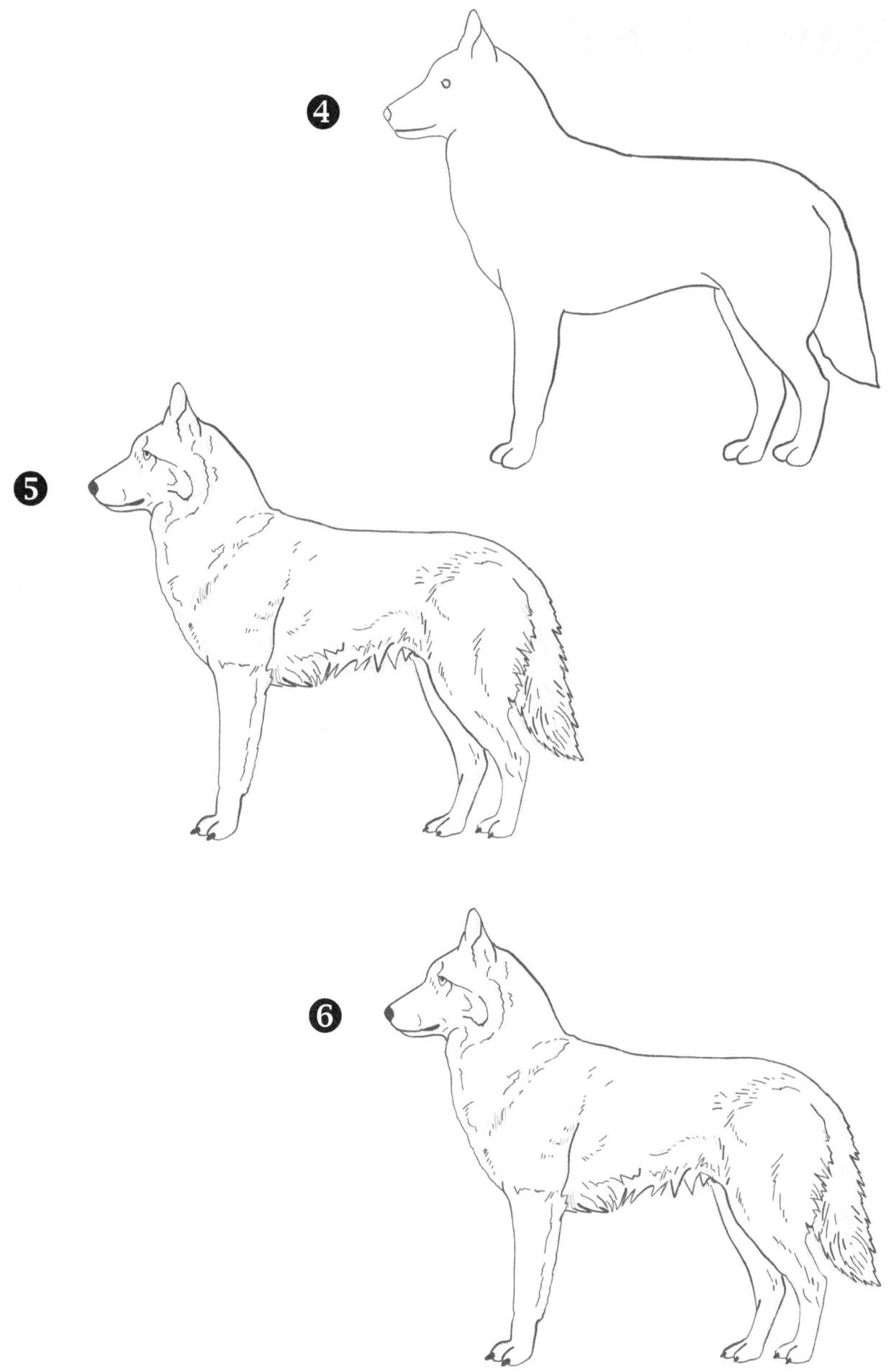

PRACTICE

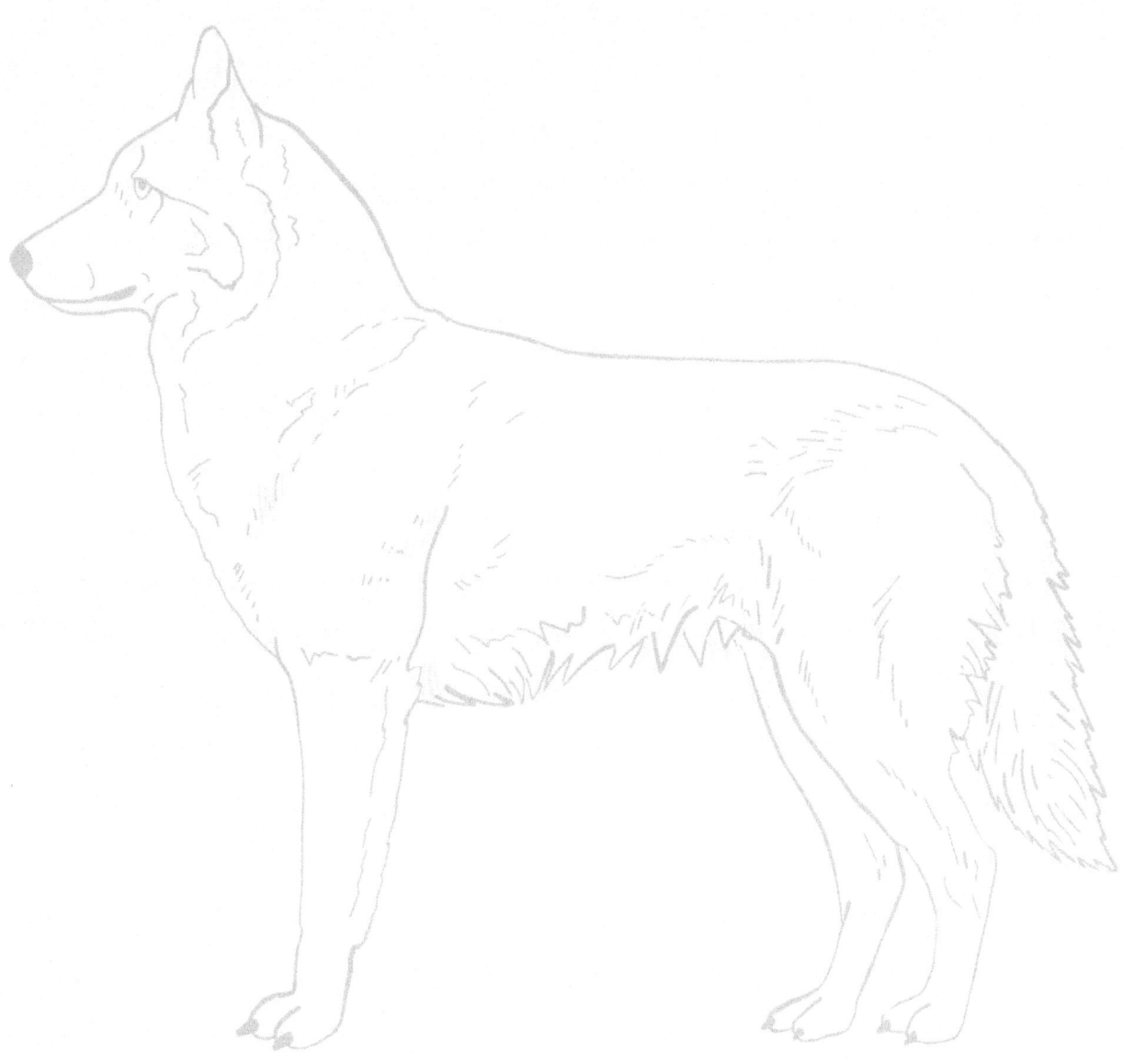

This page intentionally left blank as the back of the practice page

DRAWING AN ELEPHANT

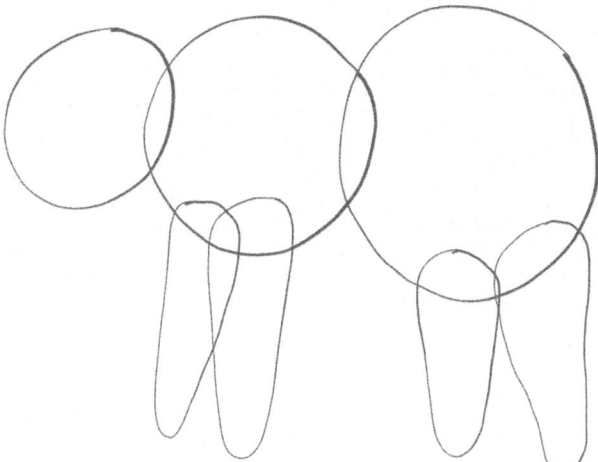

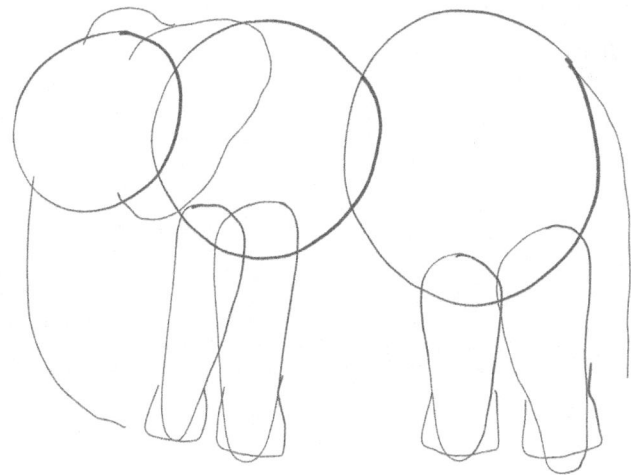

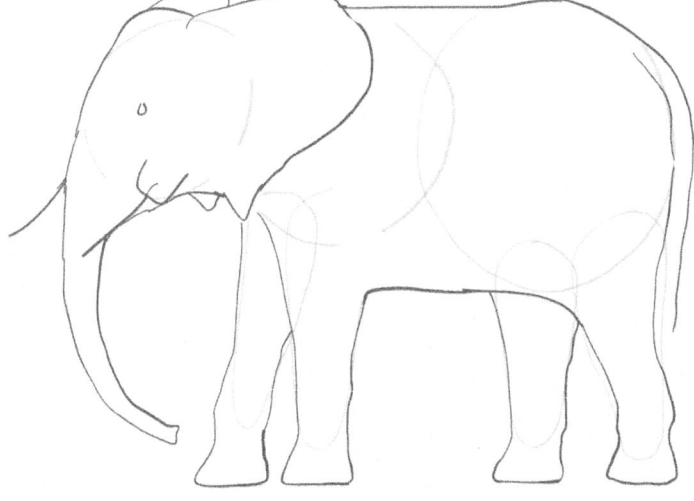

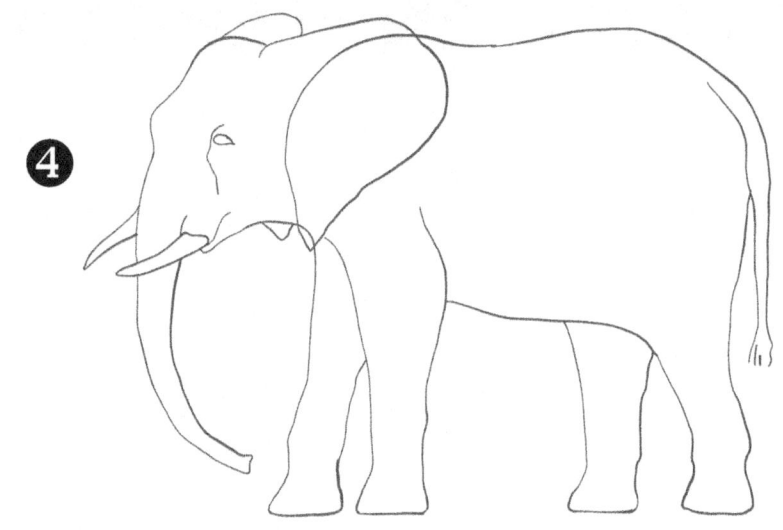

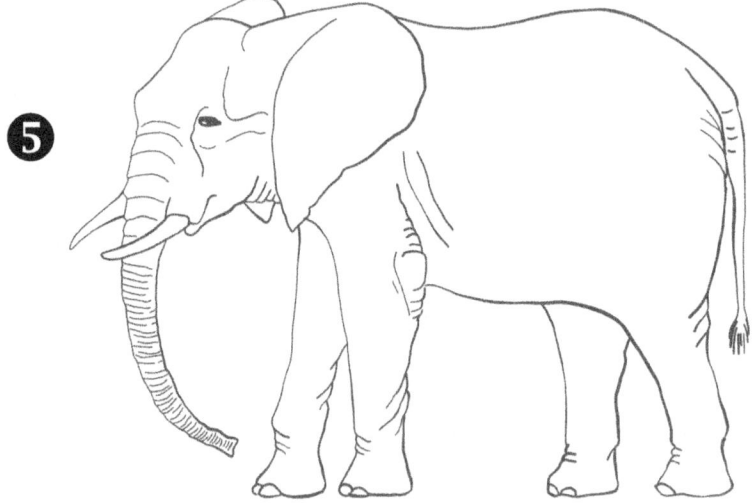

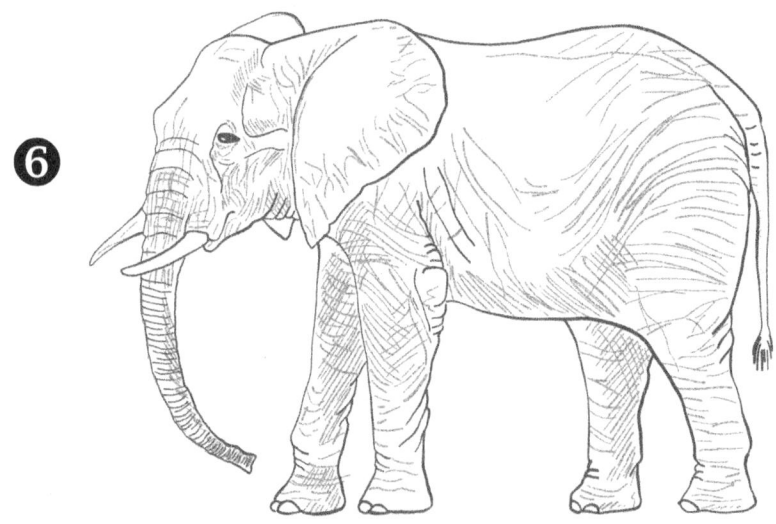

PRACTICE

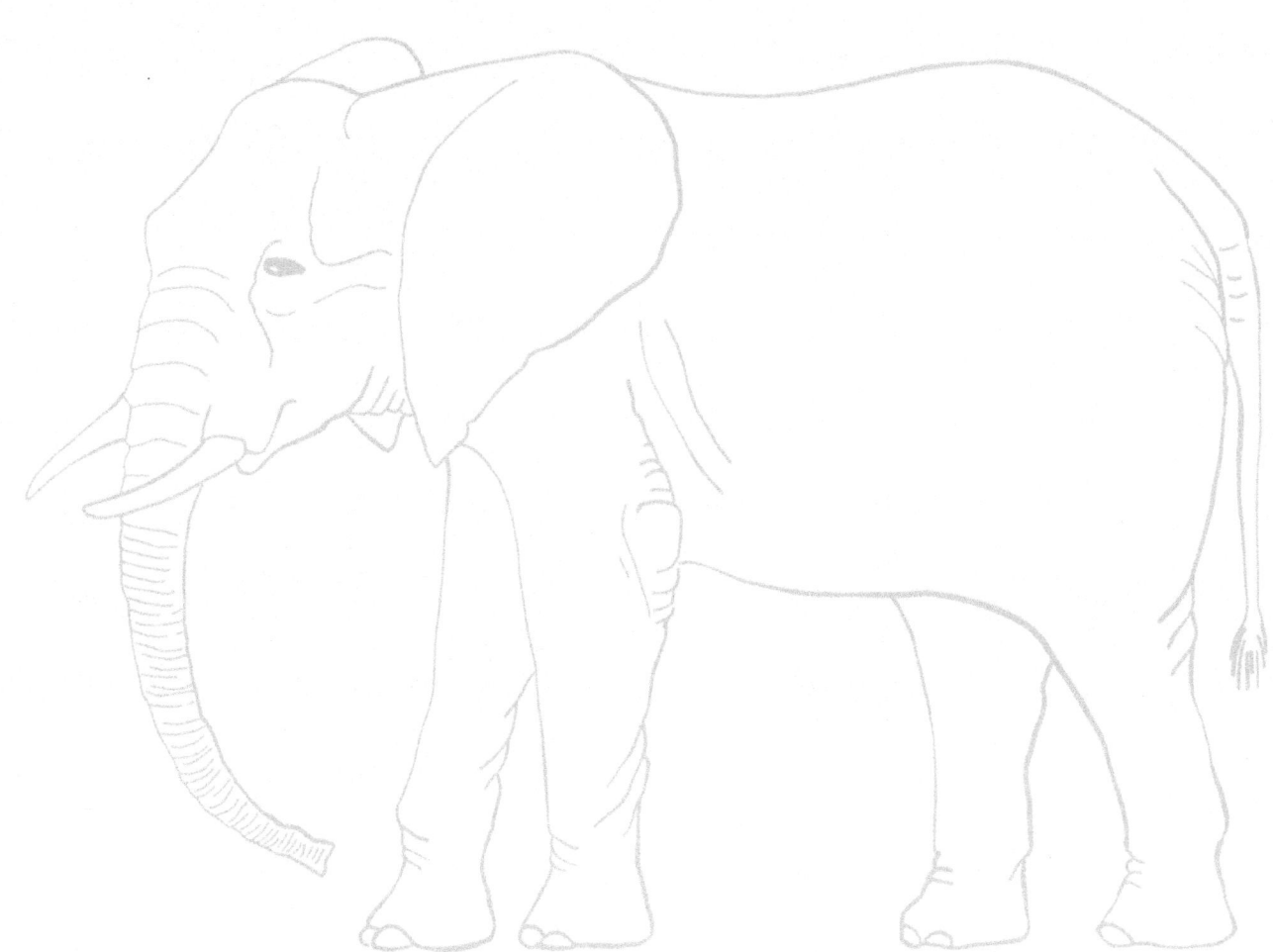

This page intentionally left blank as the back of the practice page

DRAWING A PENGUIN

①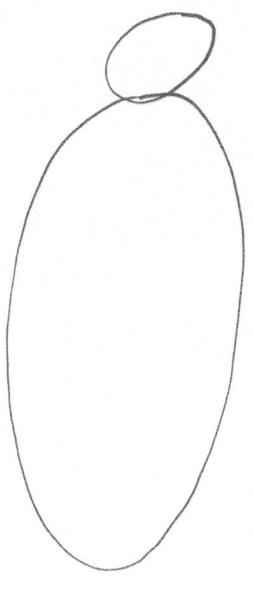

②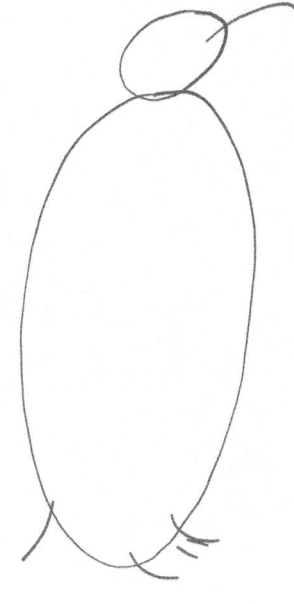

③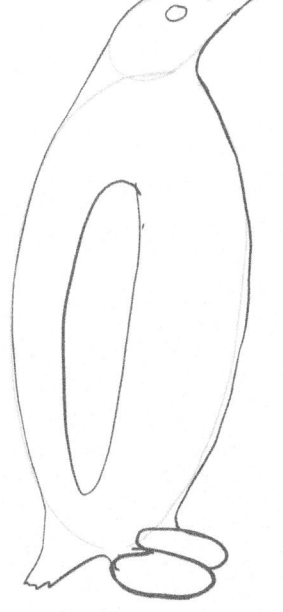

4

5

6

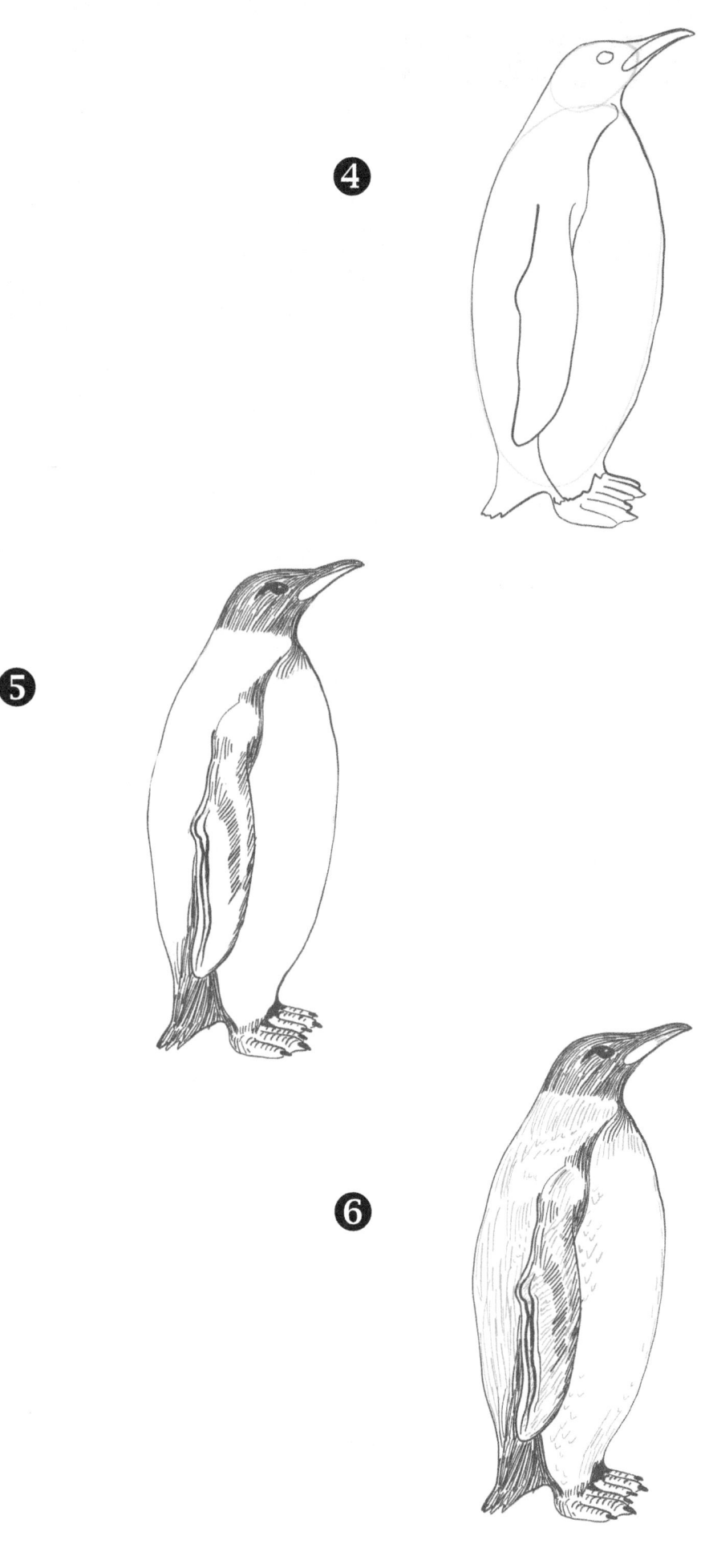

PRACTICE

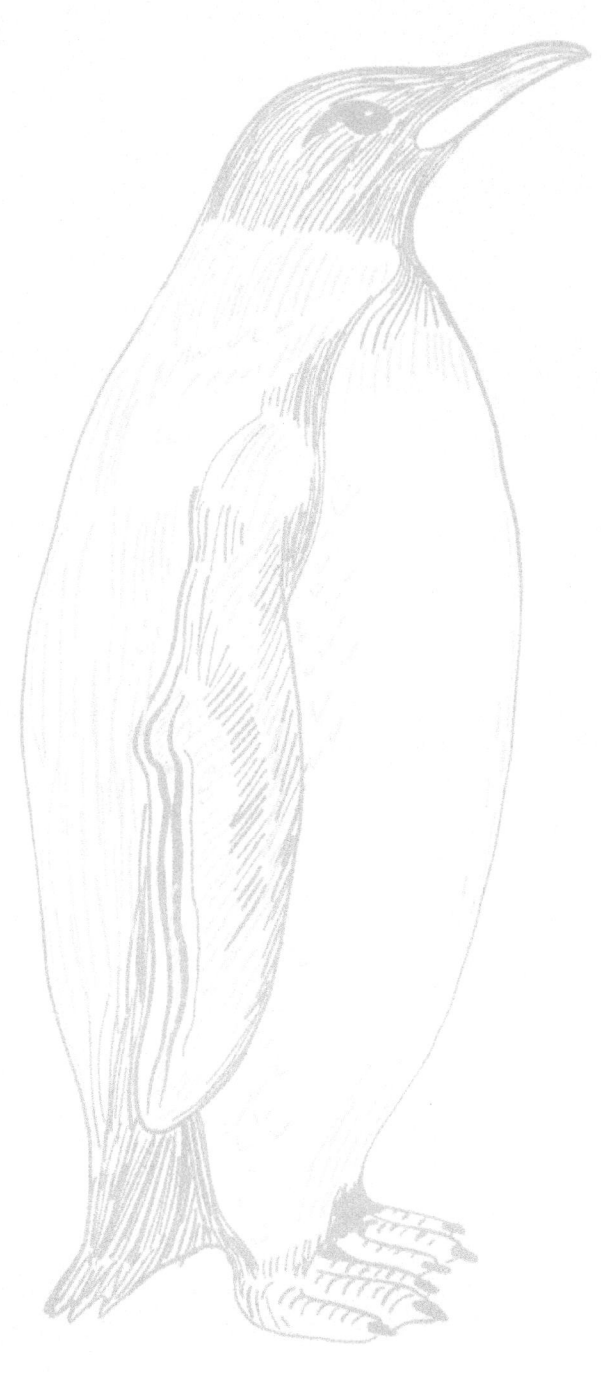

This page intentionally left blank as the back of the practice page

DRAWING A DOLPHIN

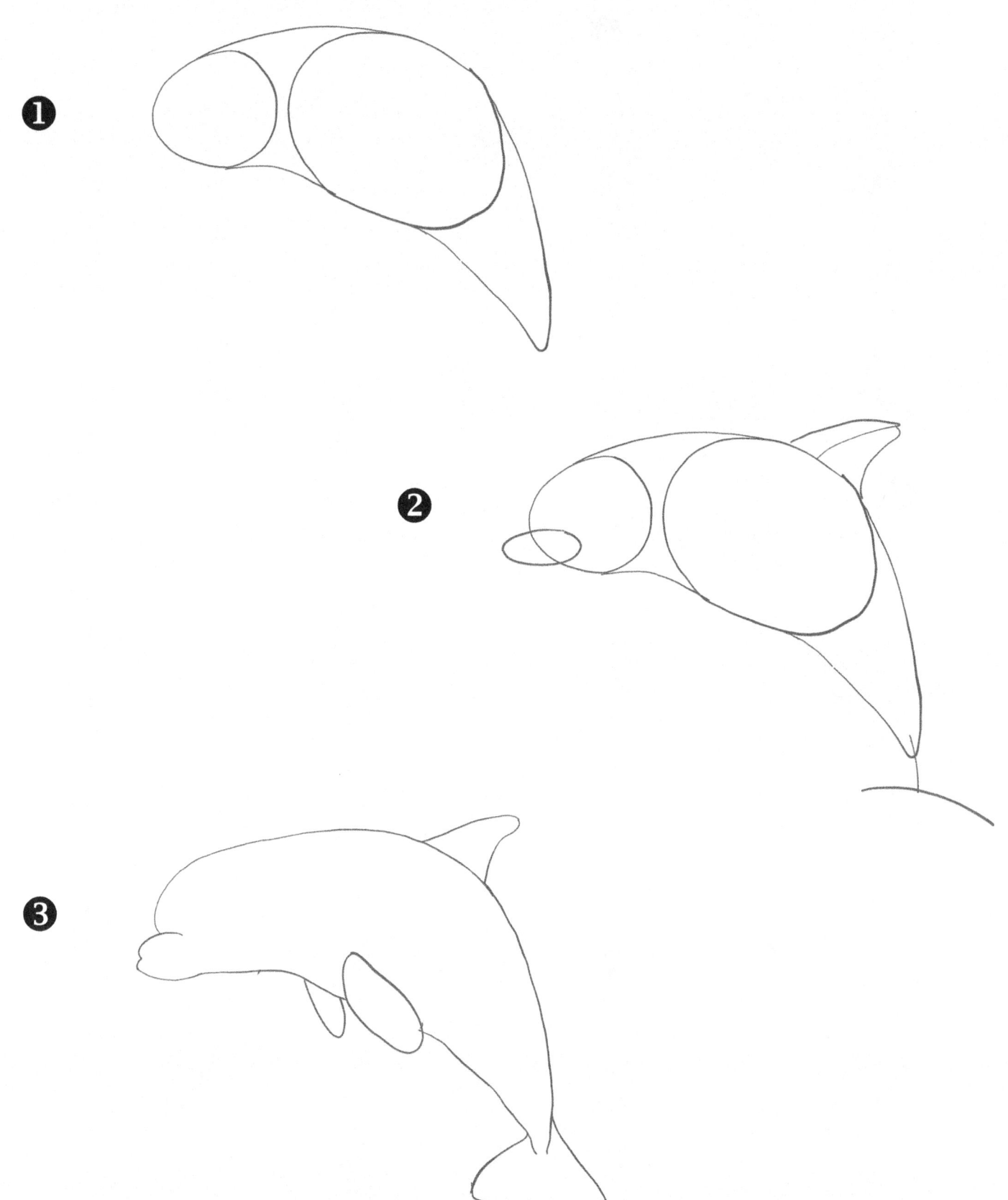

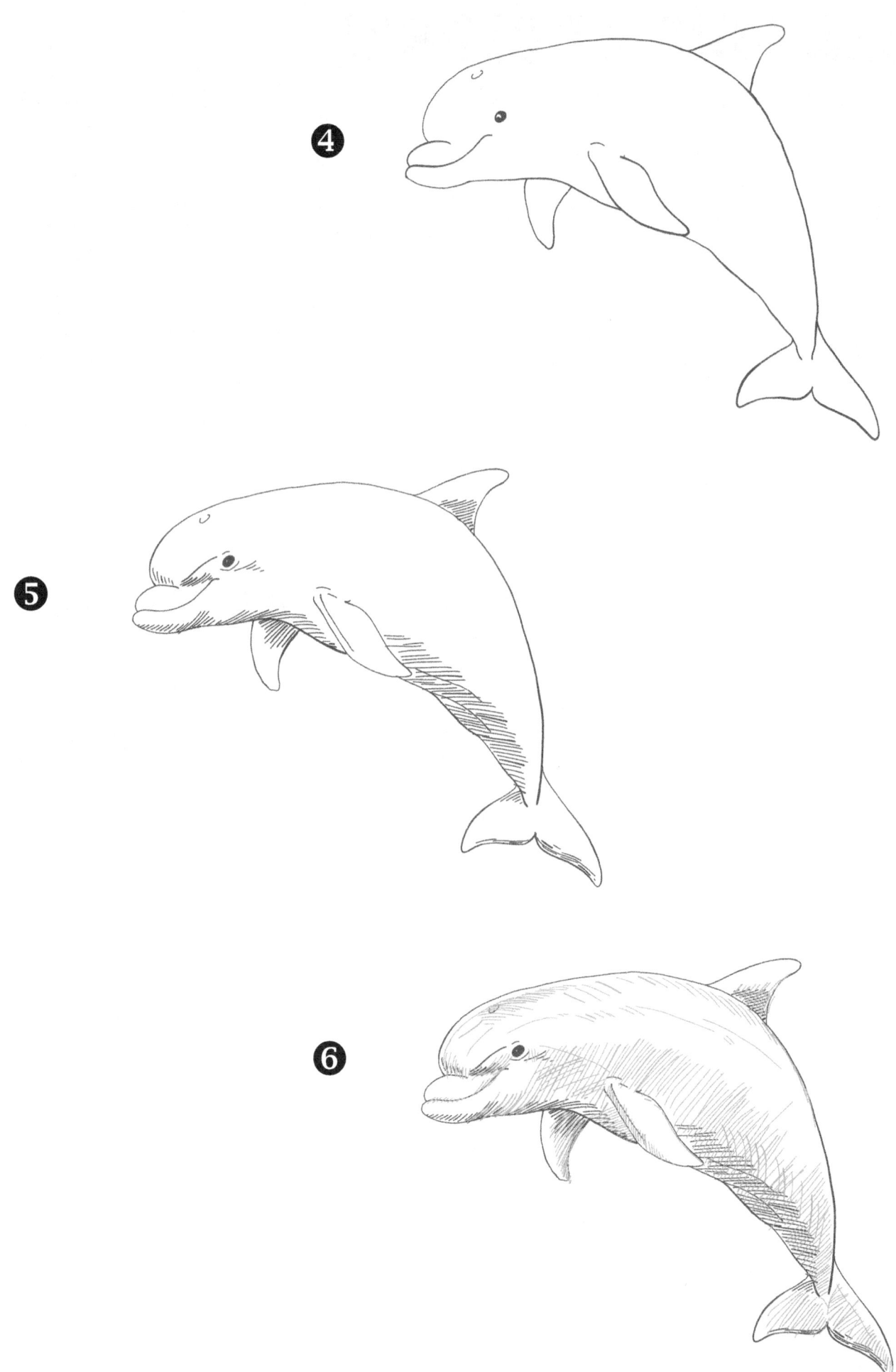

PRACTICE

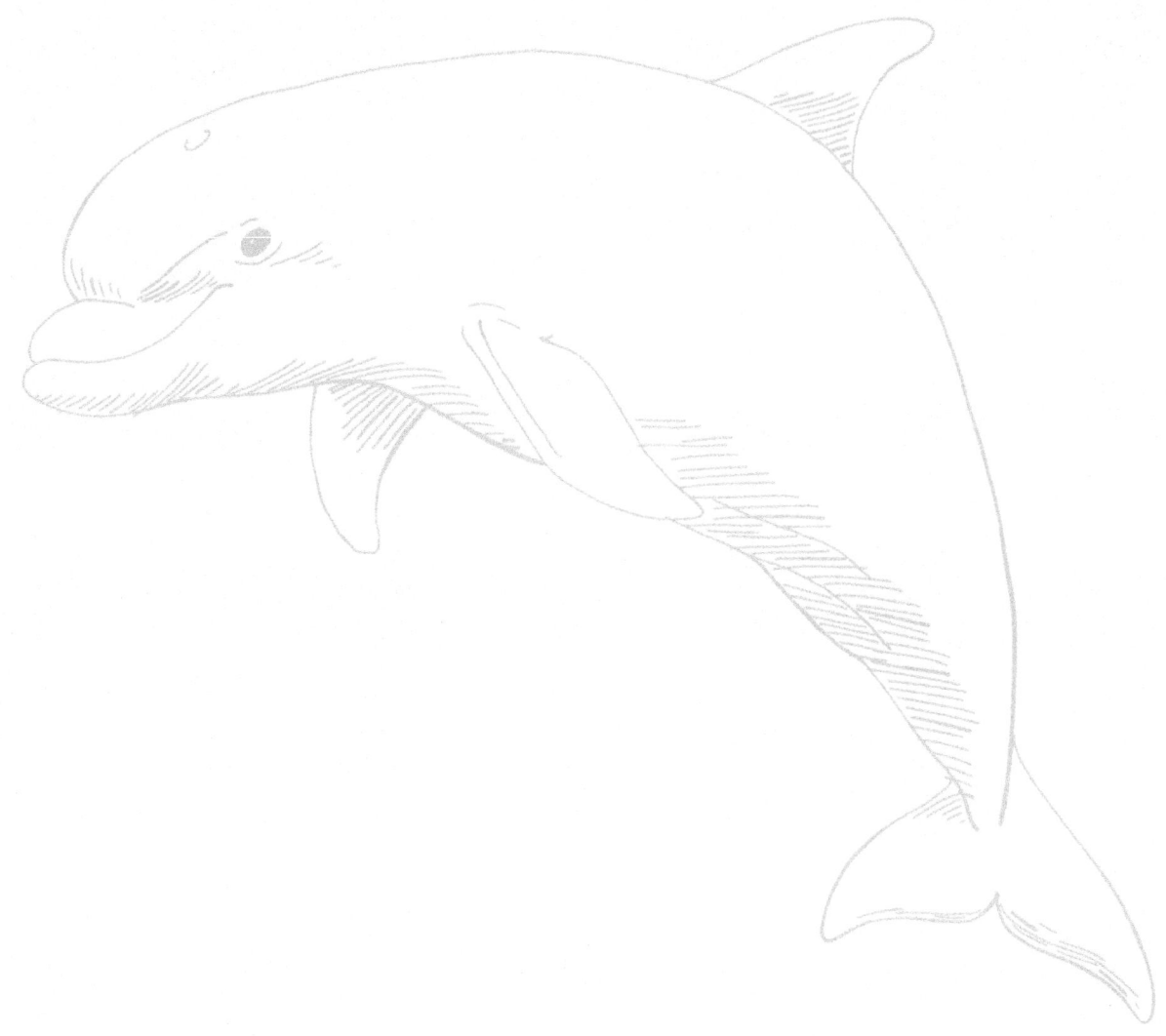

This page intentionally left blank as the back of the practice page

DRAWING A RABBIT

 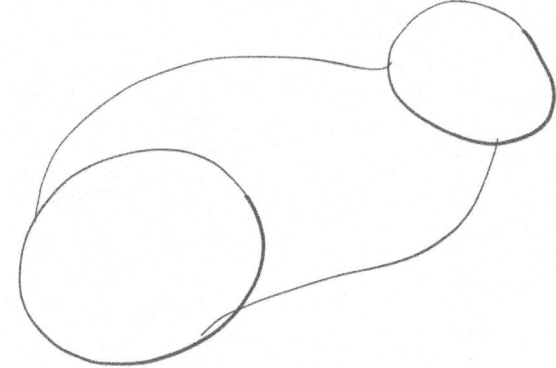

 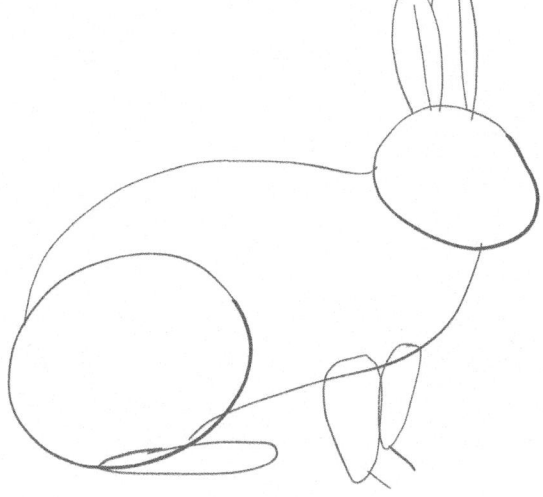

 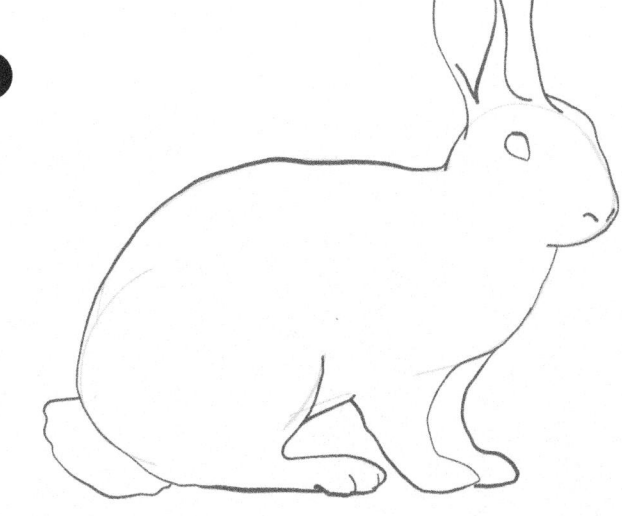

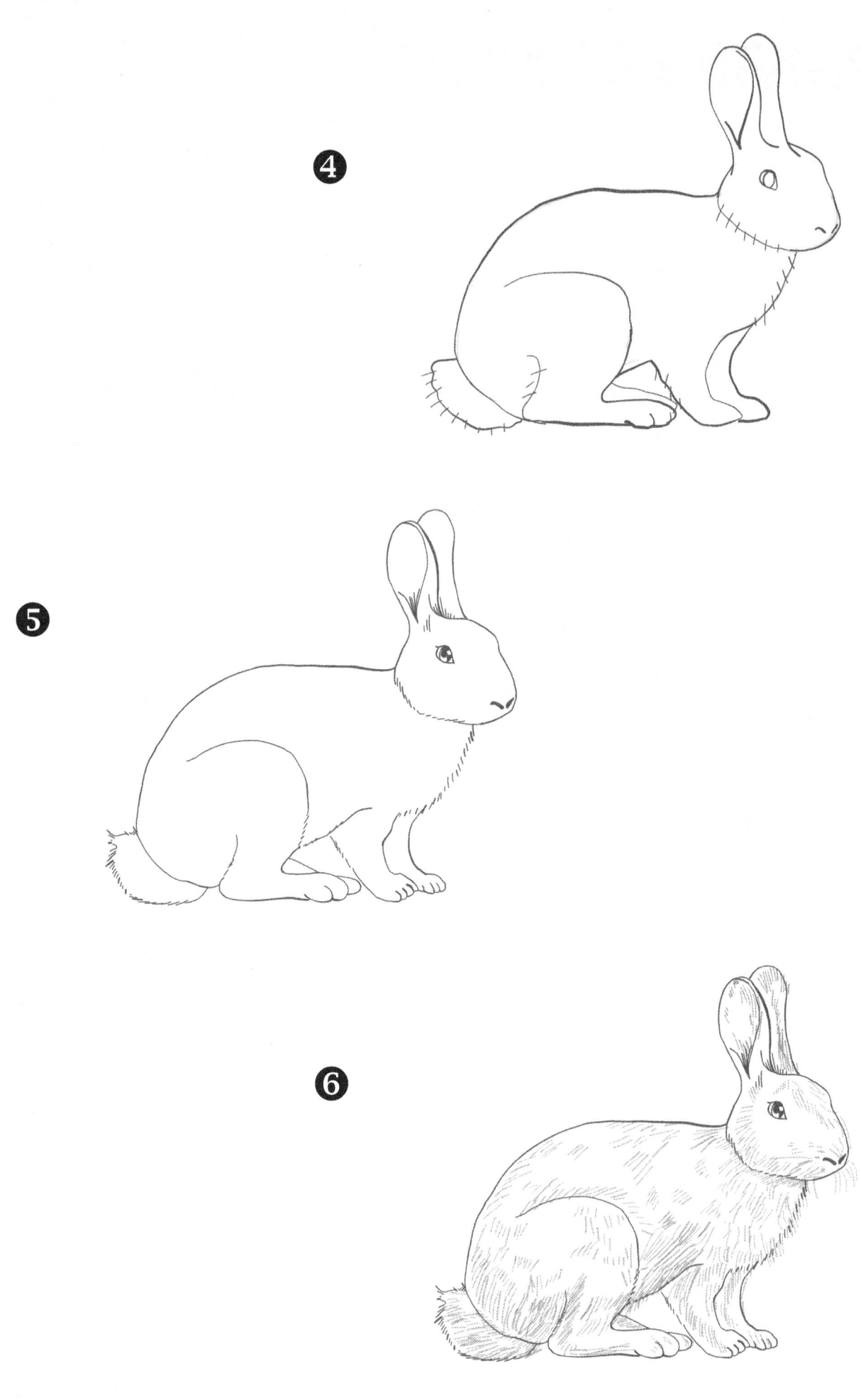

PRACTICE

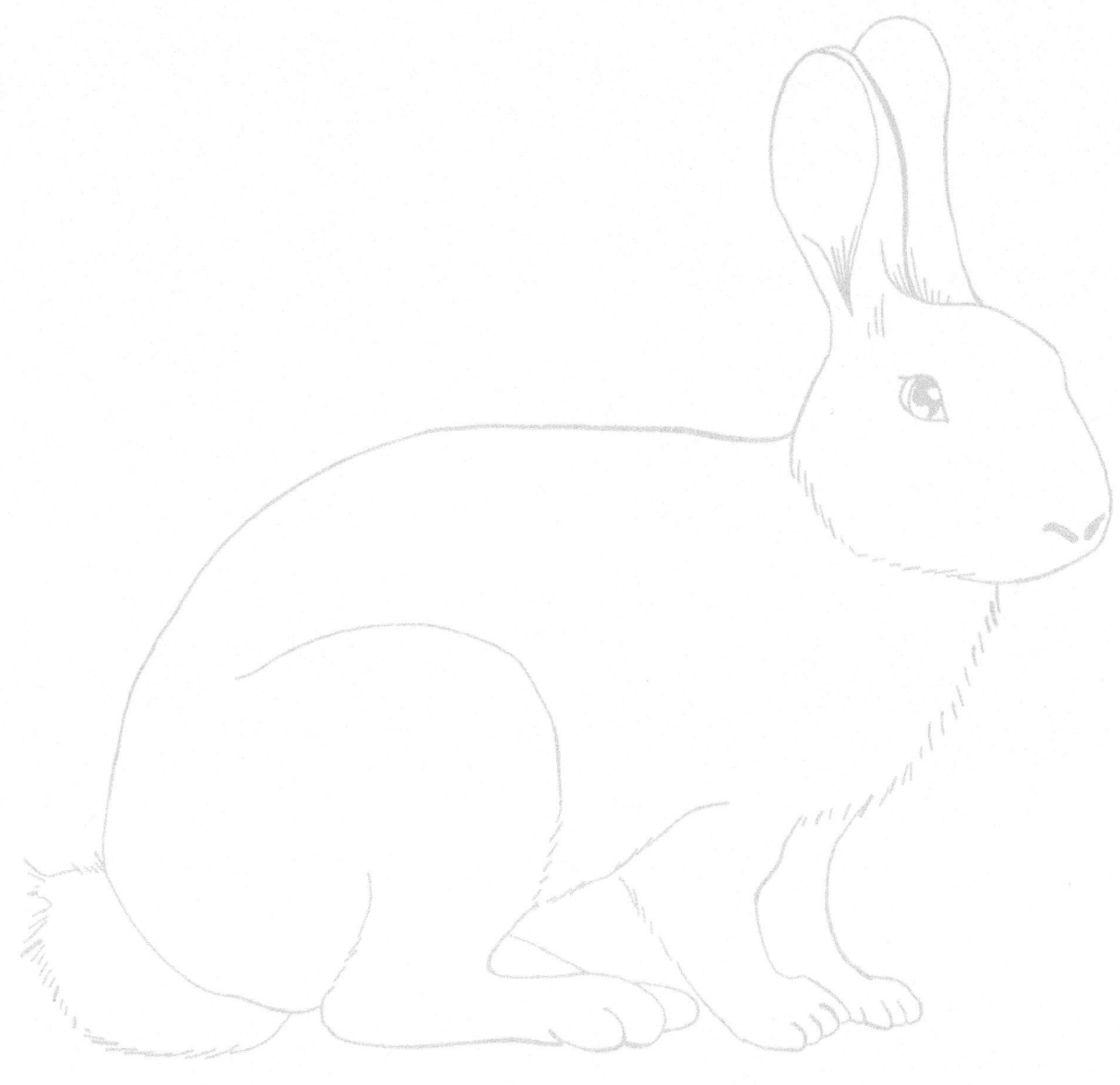

This page intentionally left blank as the back of the practice page

DRAWING A FROG

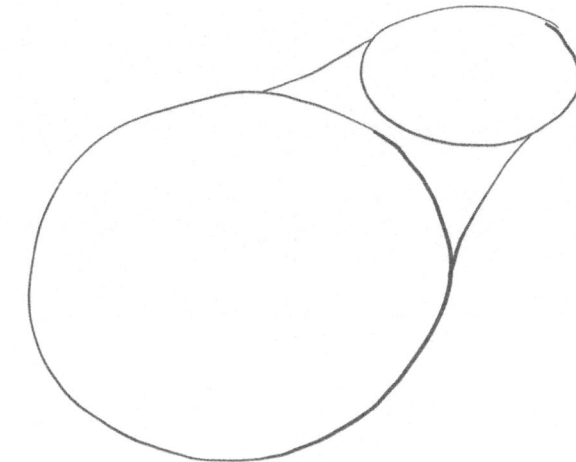

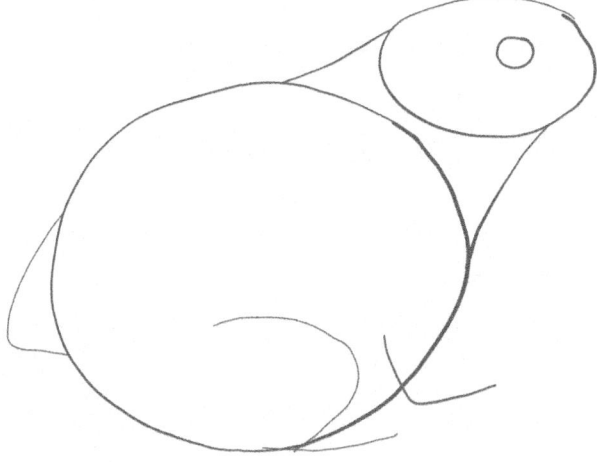

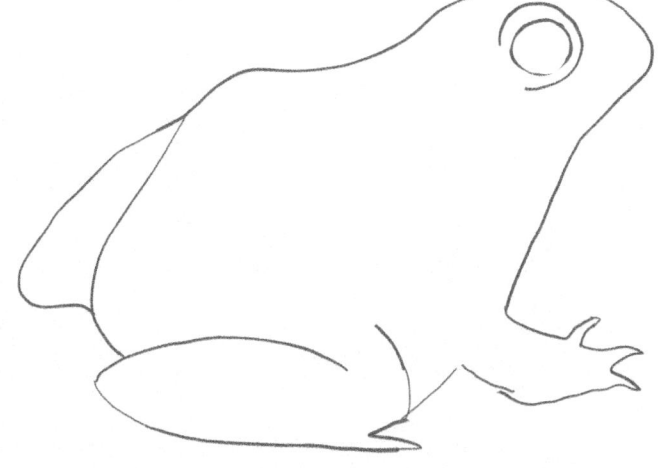

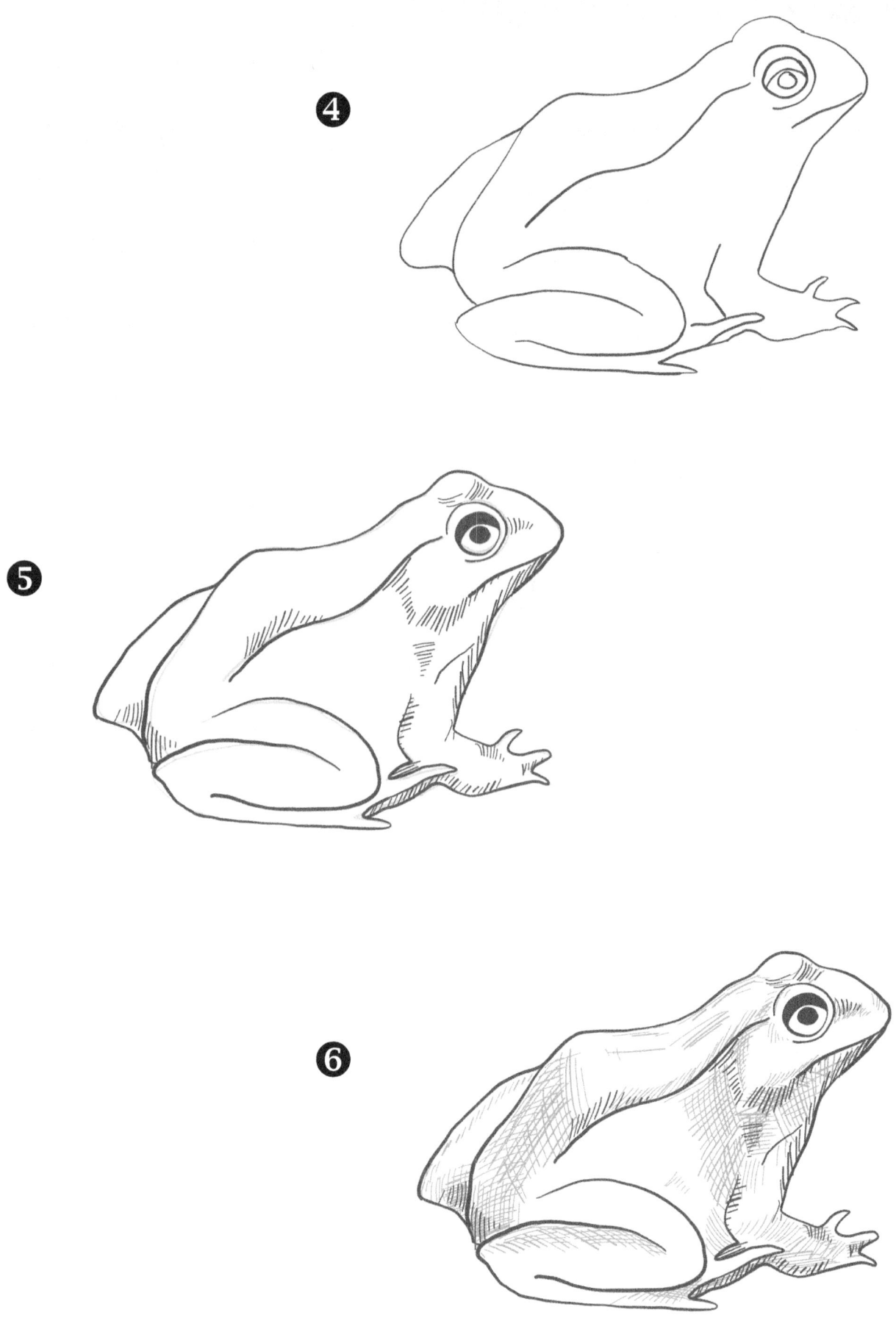

PRACTICE

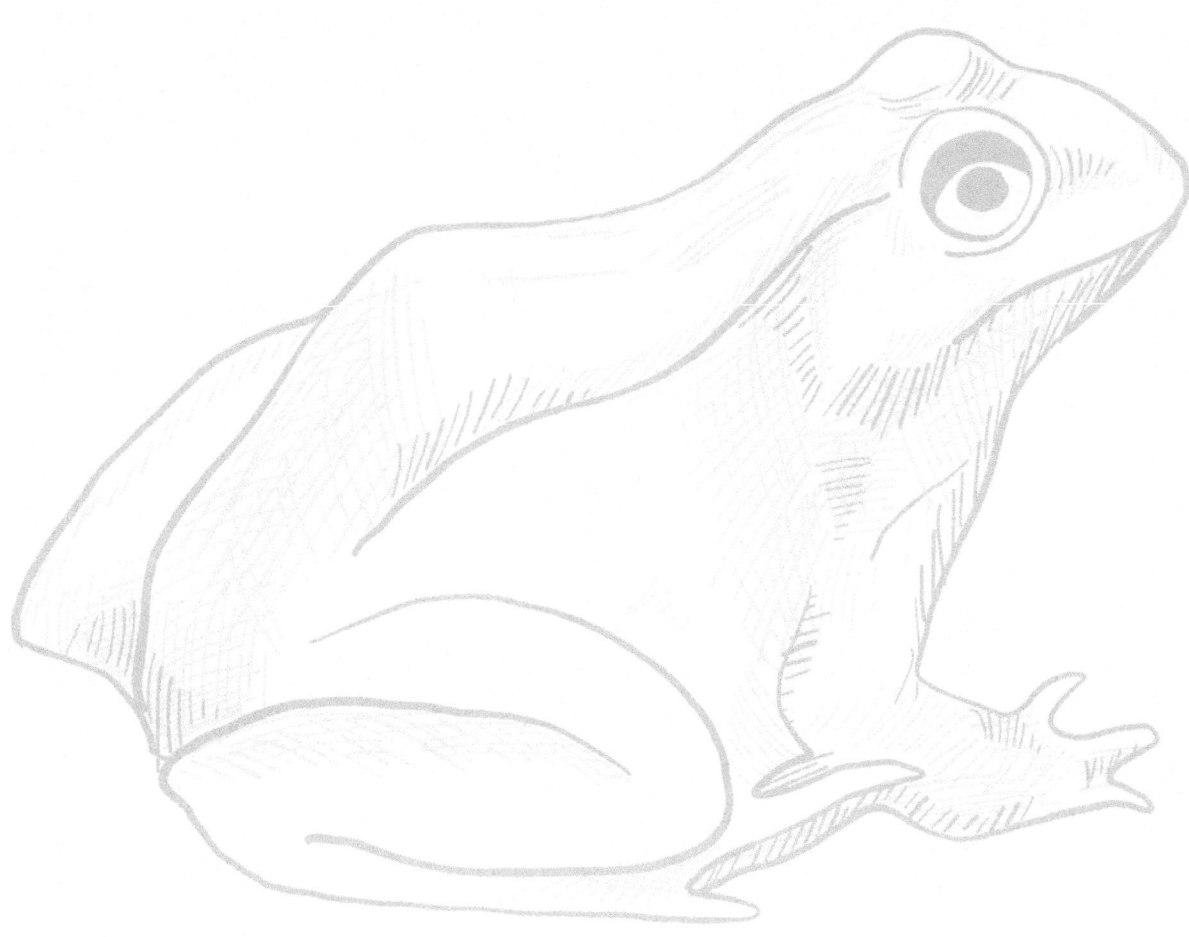

This page intentionally left blank as the back of the practice page

DRAWING A PIG

1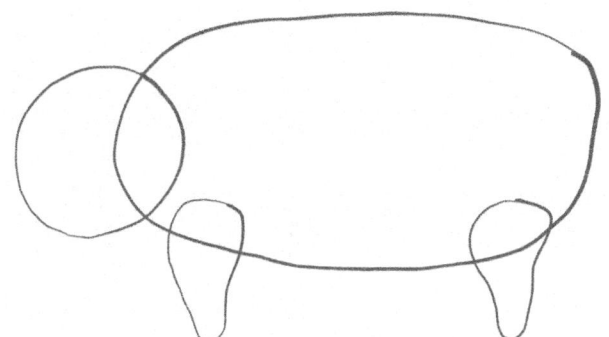

2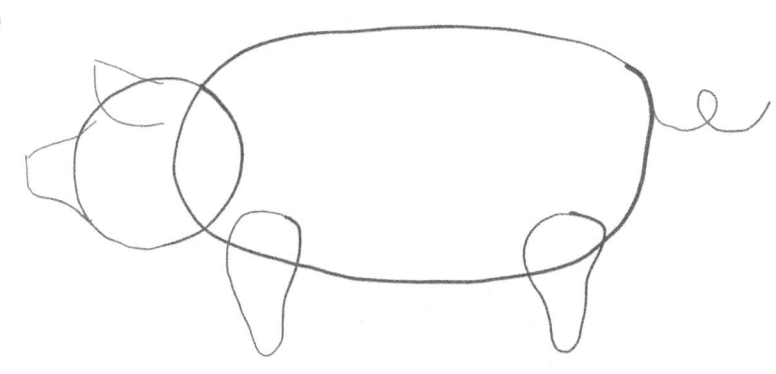

3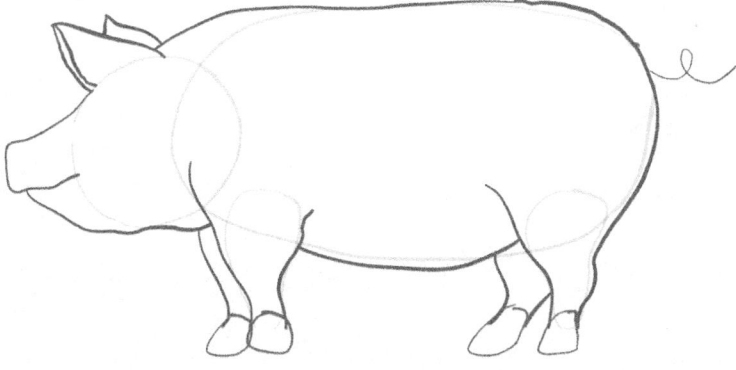

❹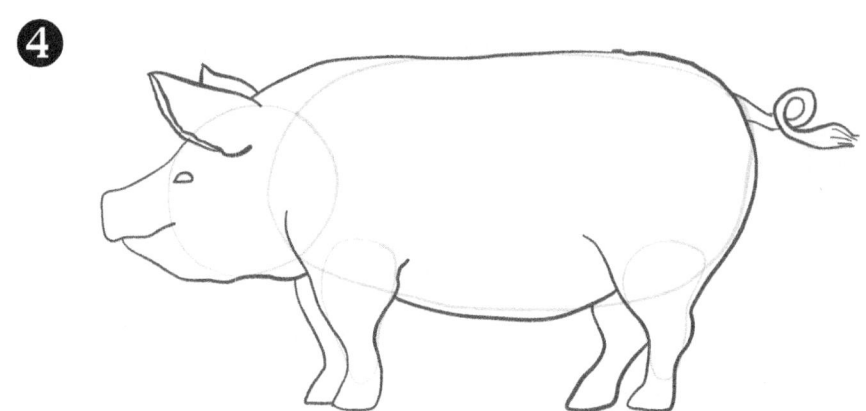

❺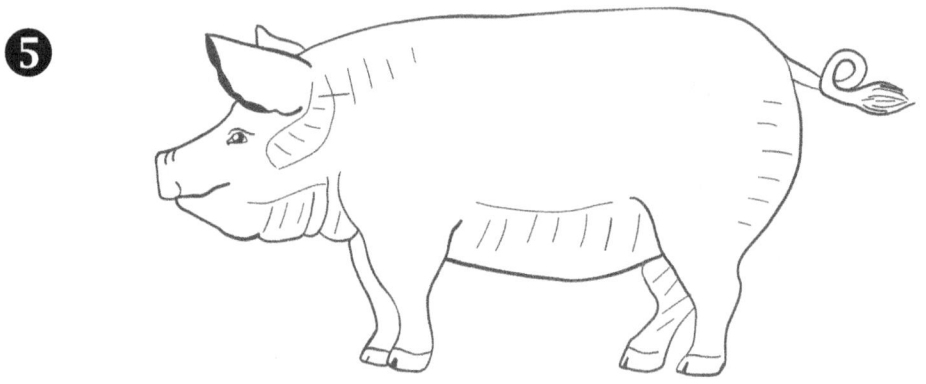

❻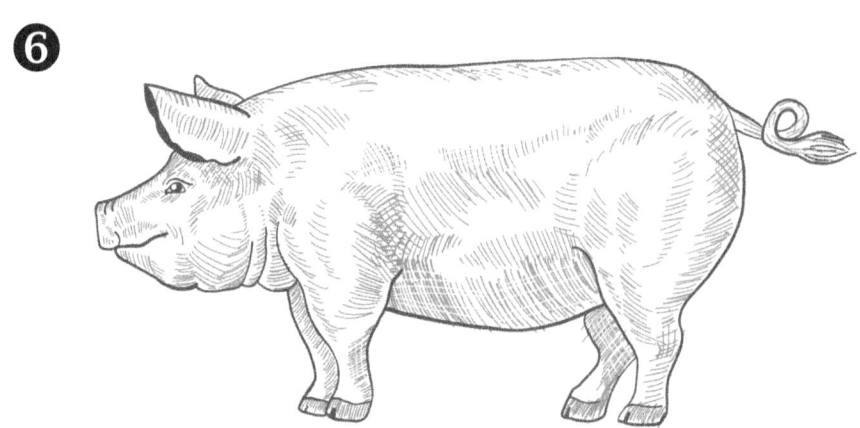

PRACTICE

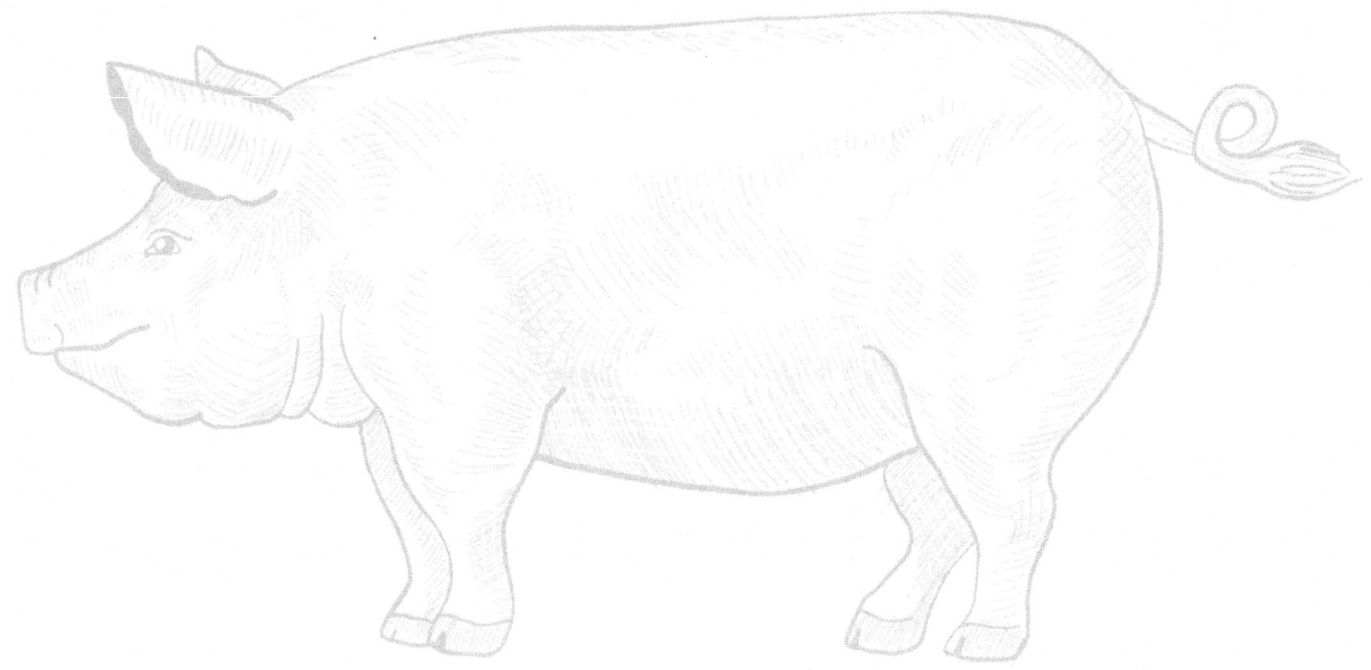

This page intentionally left blank as the back of the practice page

DRAWING A CHICKEN

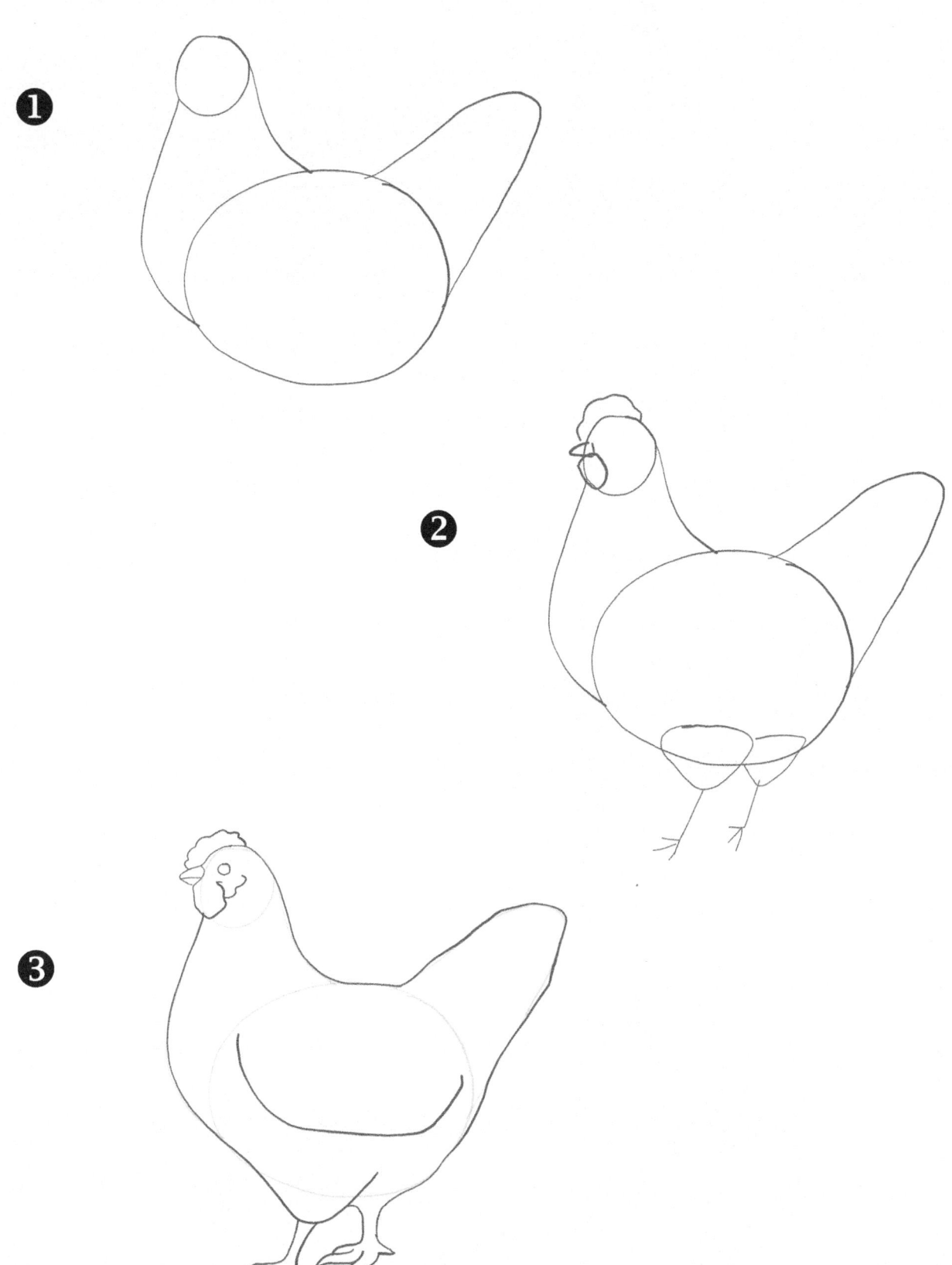

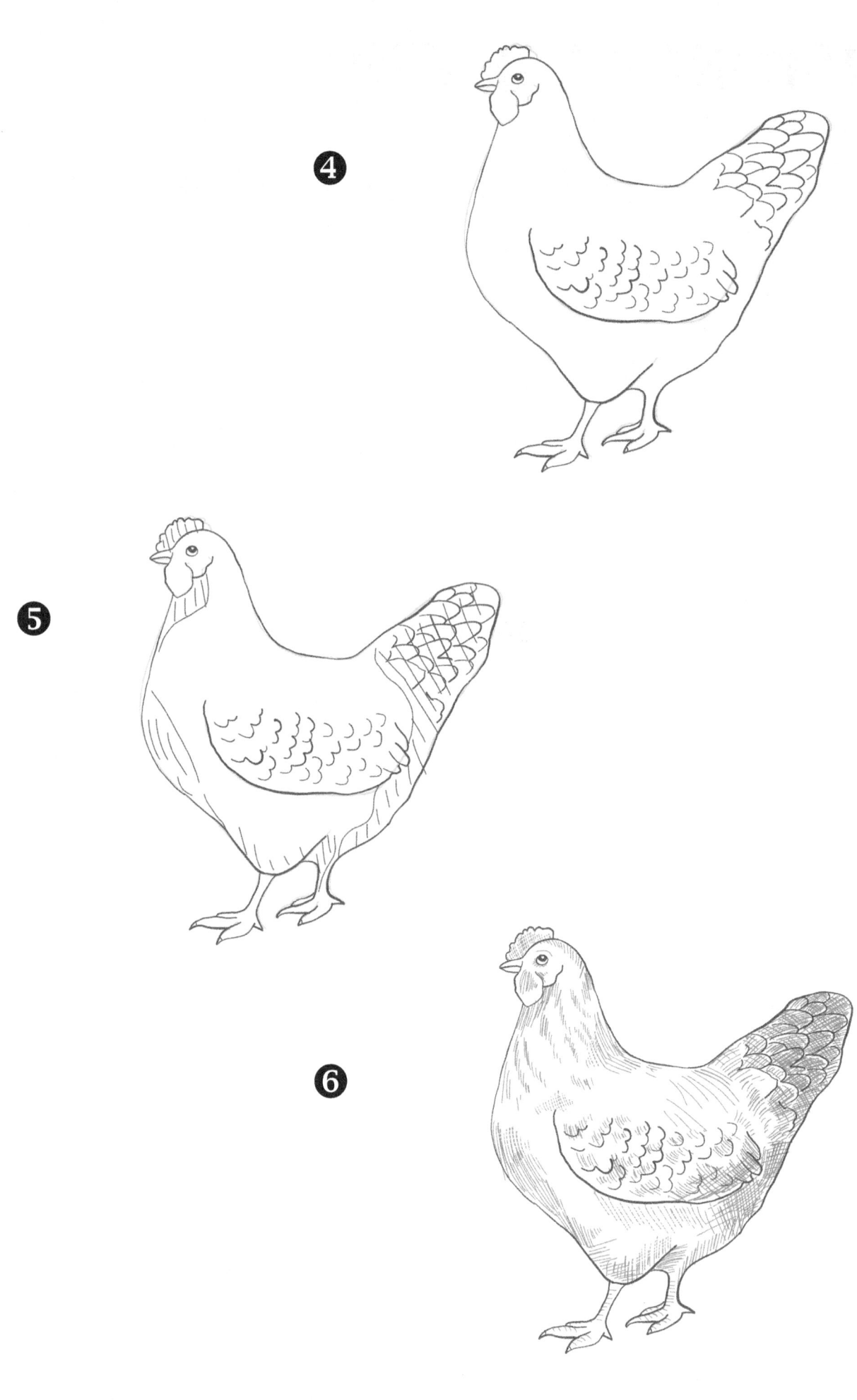

④

⑤

⑥

PRACTICE

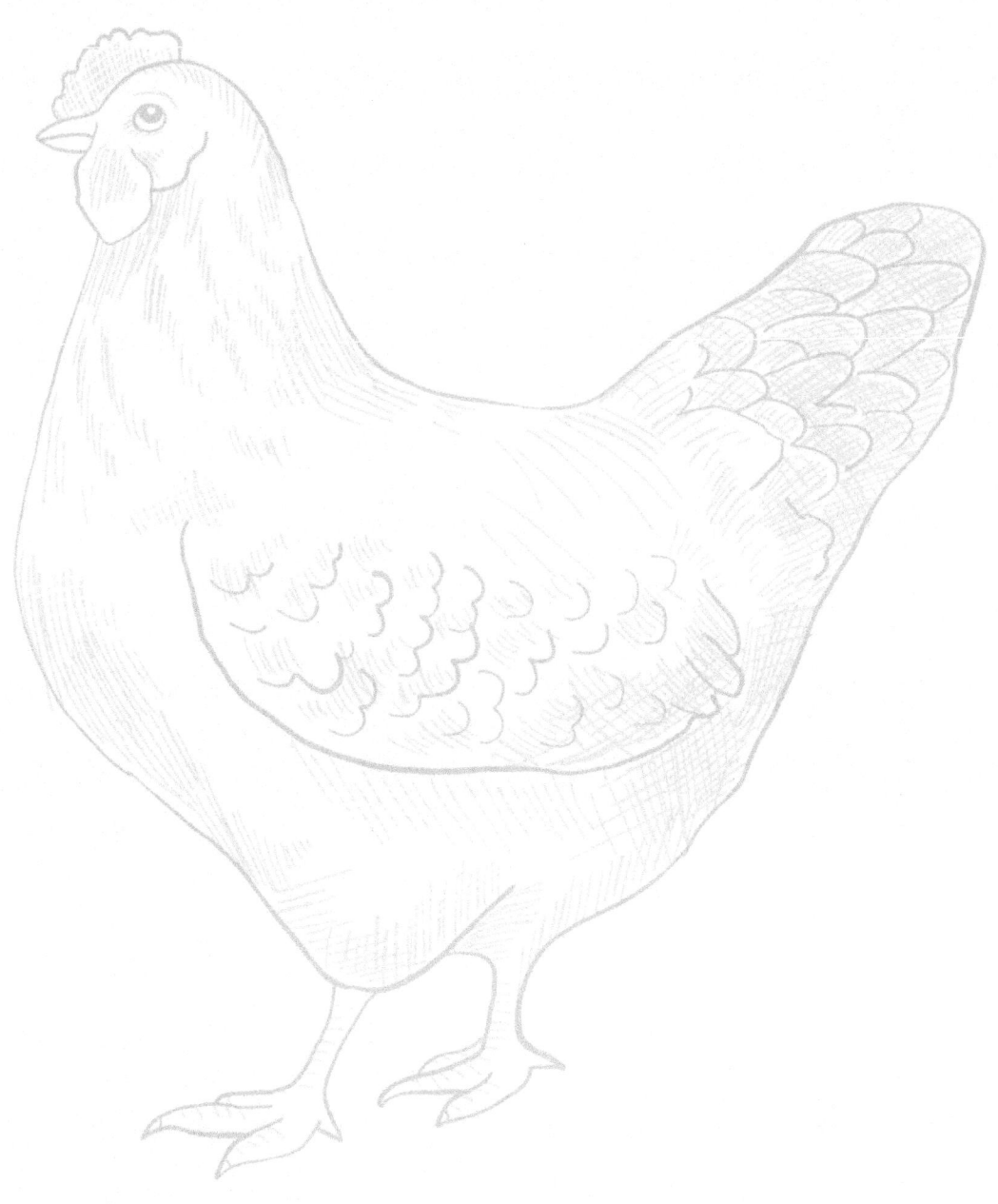

This page intentionally left blank as the back of the practice page

DRAWING A PANDA

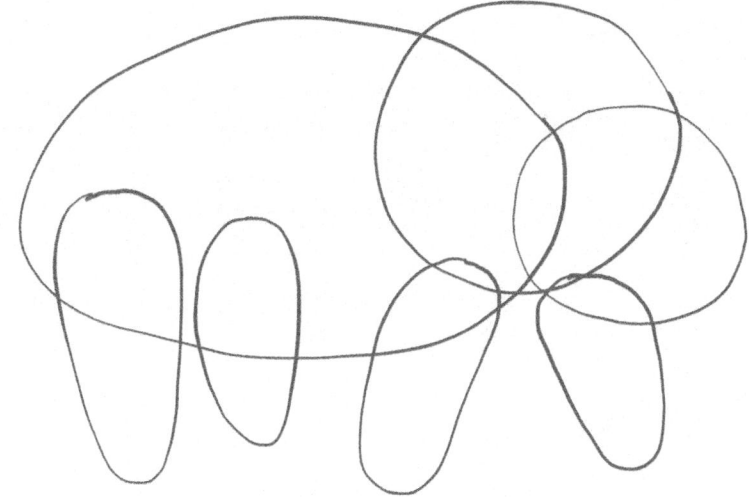

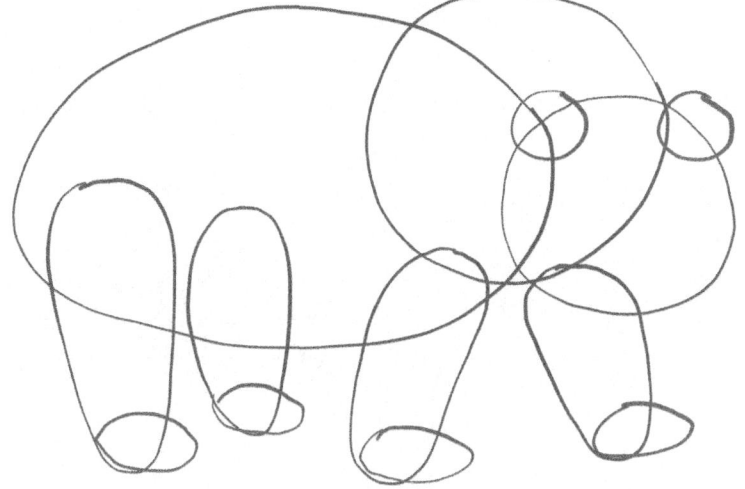

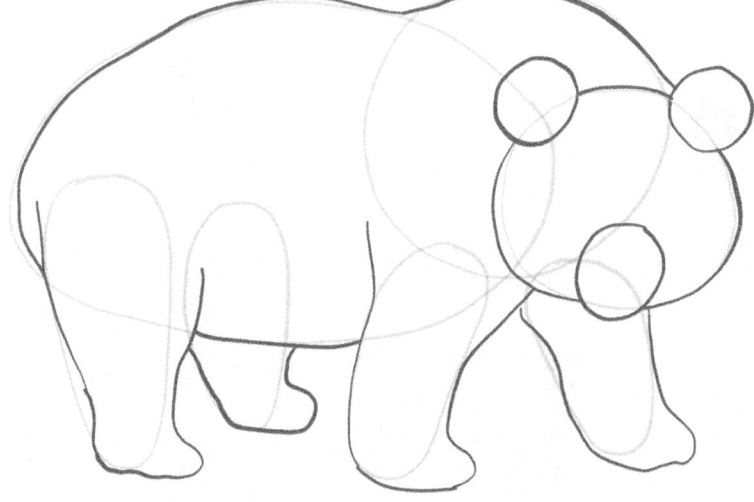

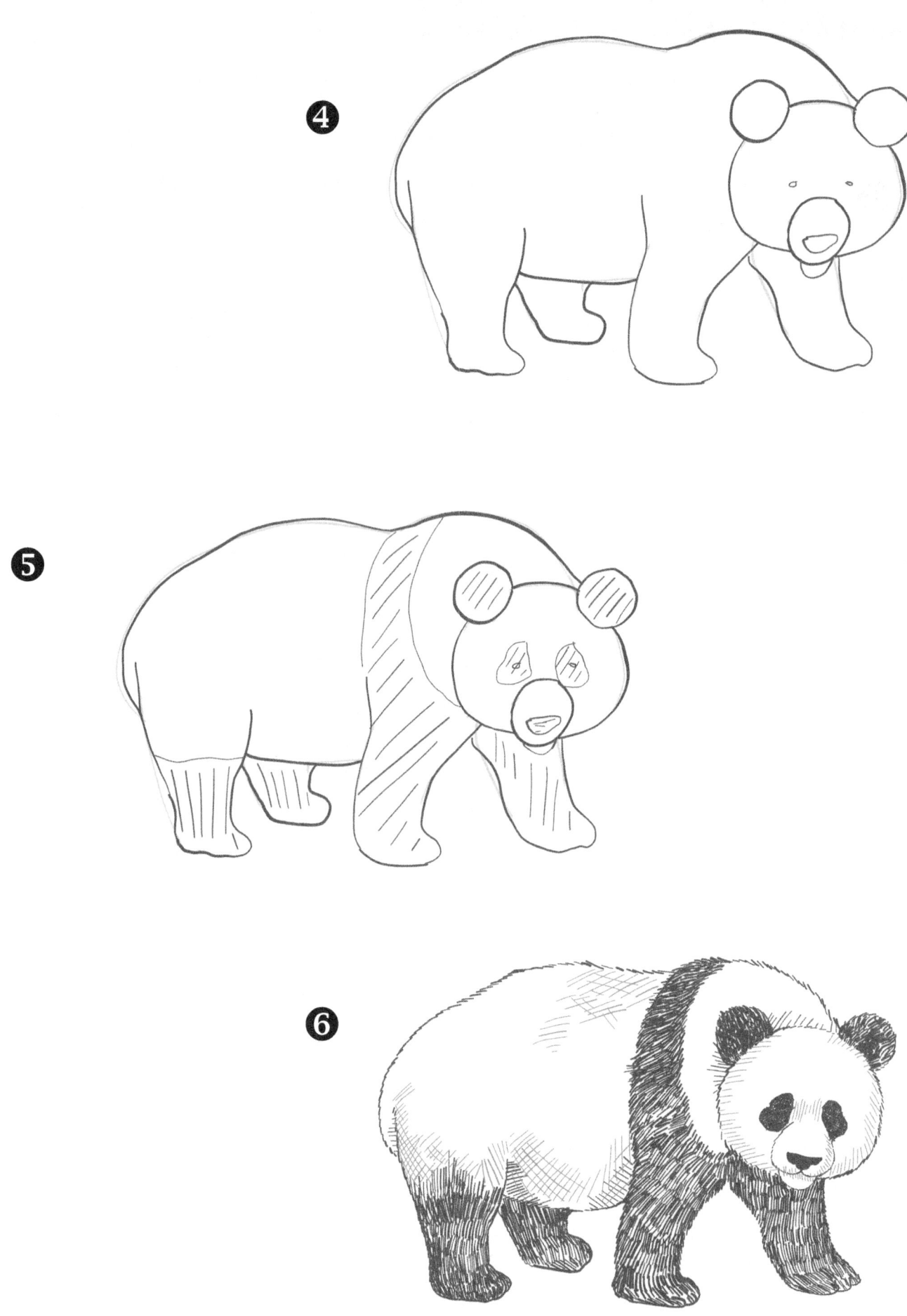

PRACTICE

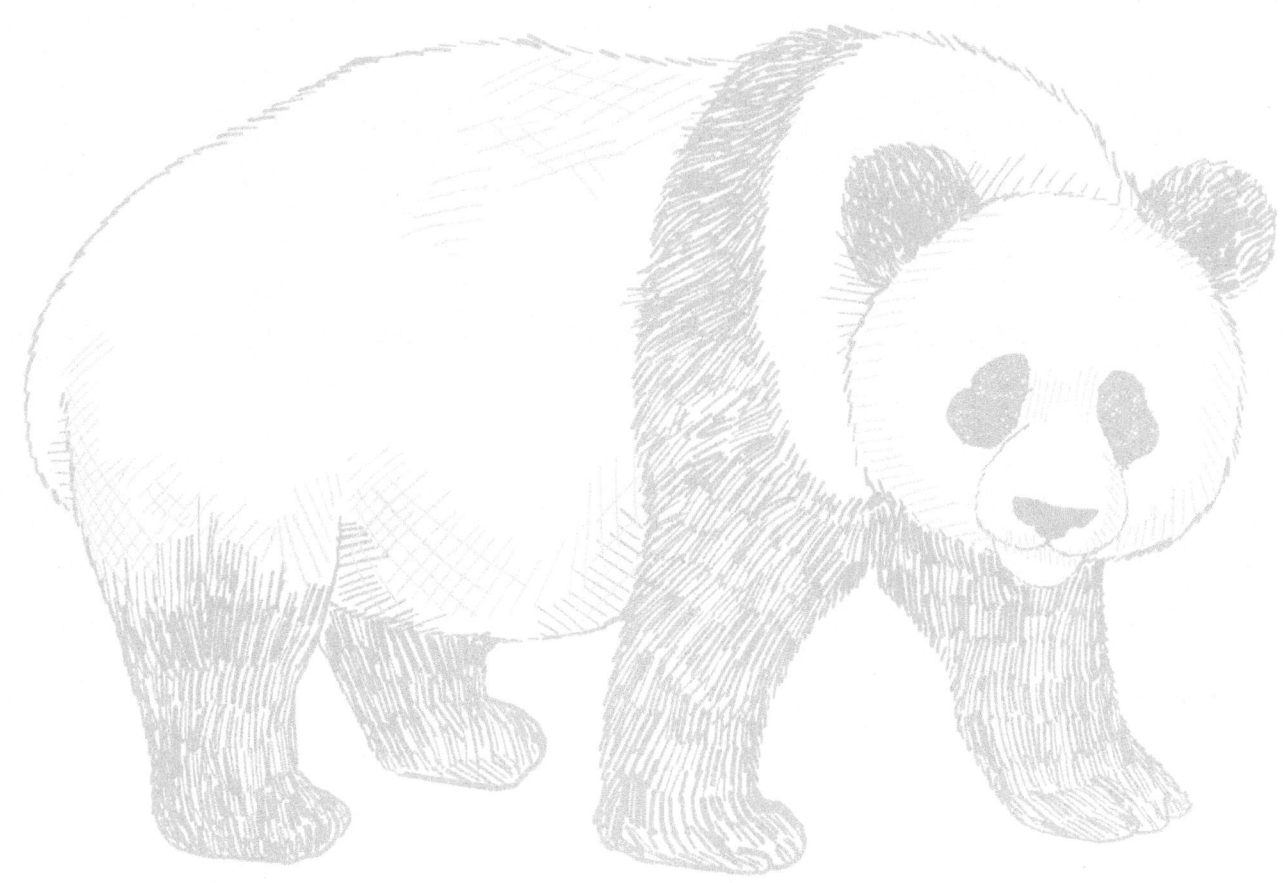

This page intentionally left blank as the back of the practice page

DRAWING A RHINOCEROS

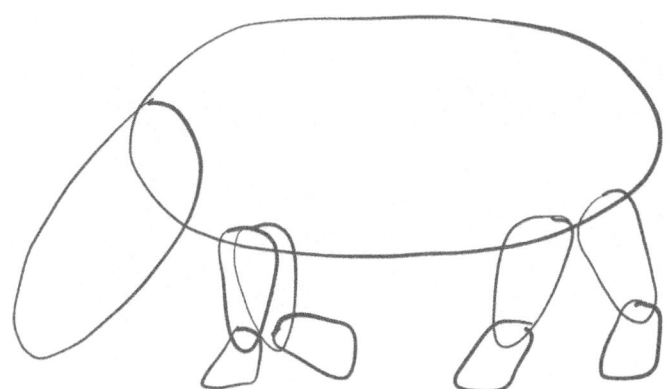

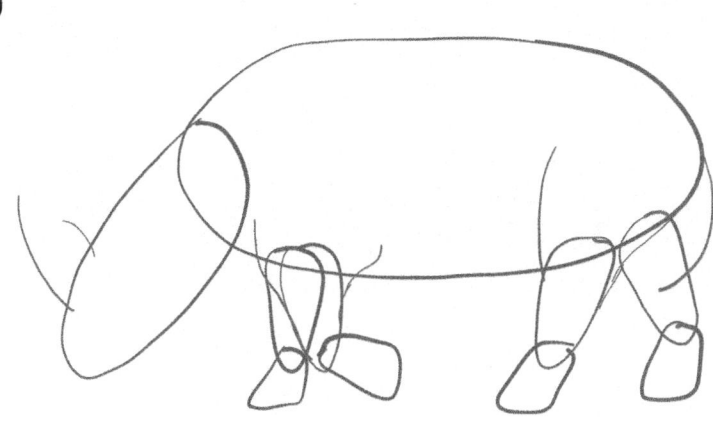

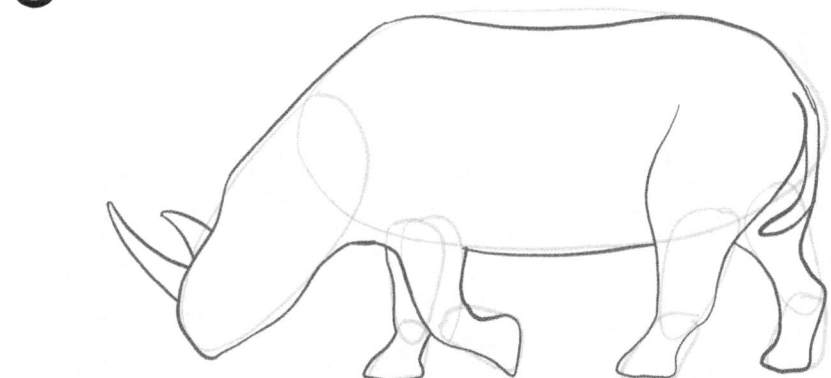

4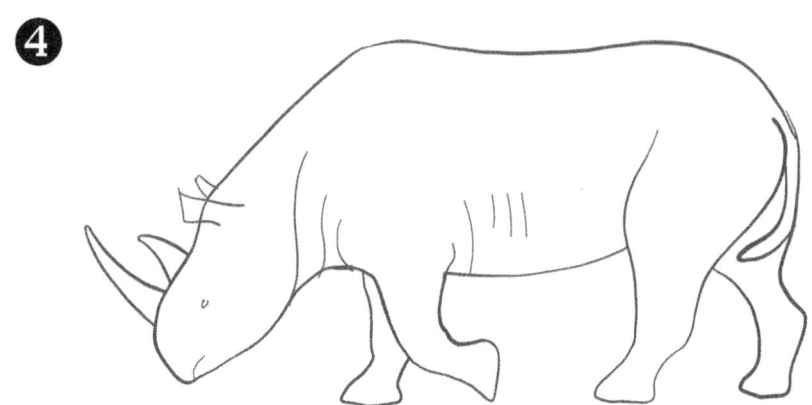

5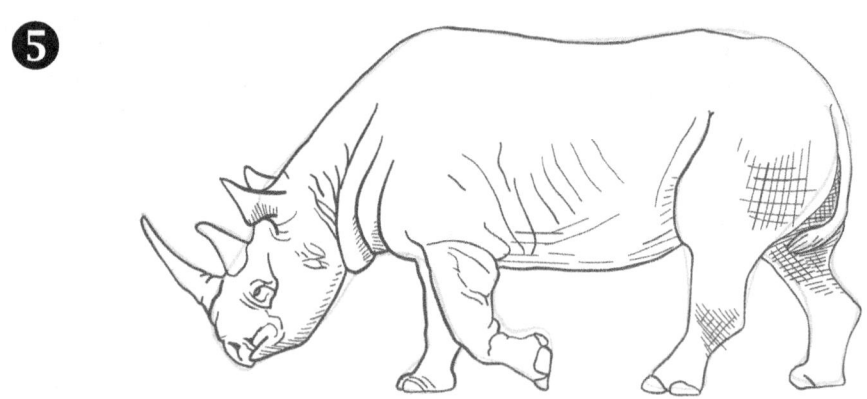

6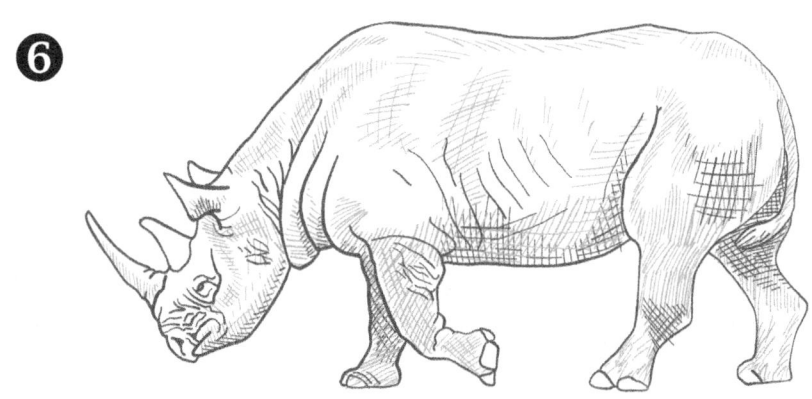

PRACTICE

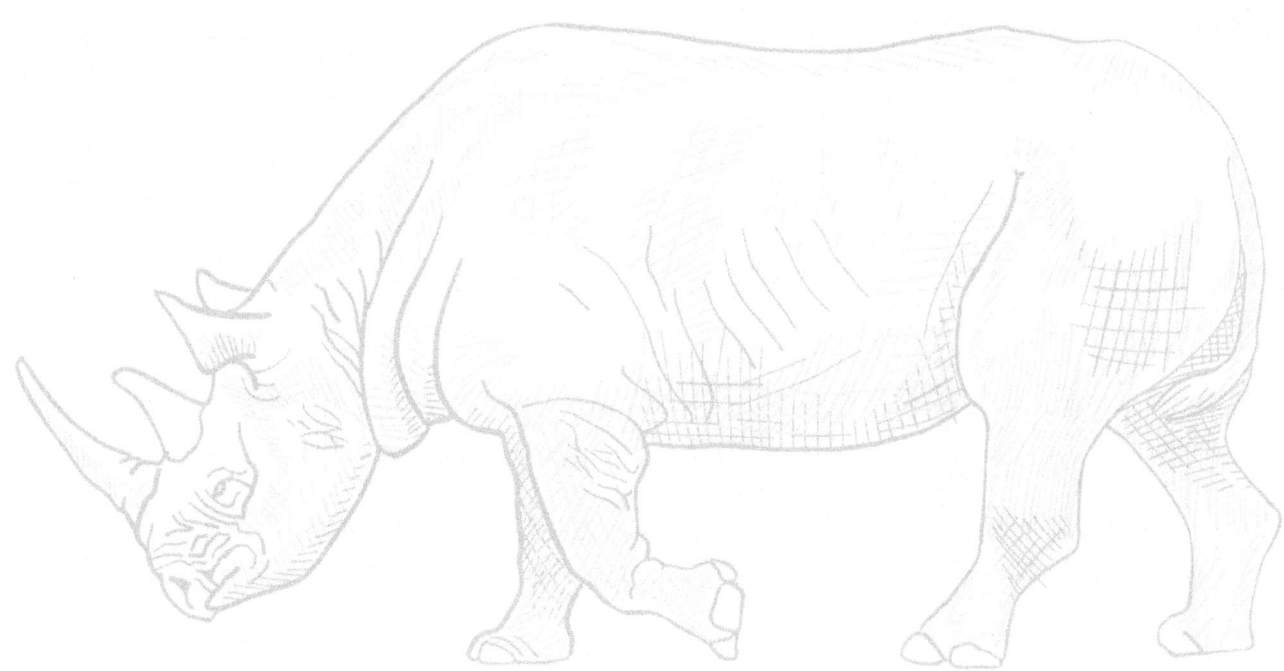

This page intentionally left blank as the back of the practice page

DRAWING A BEAR

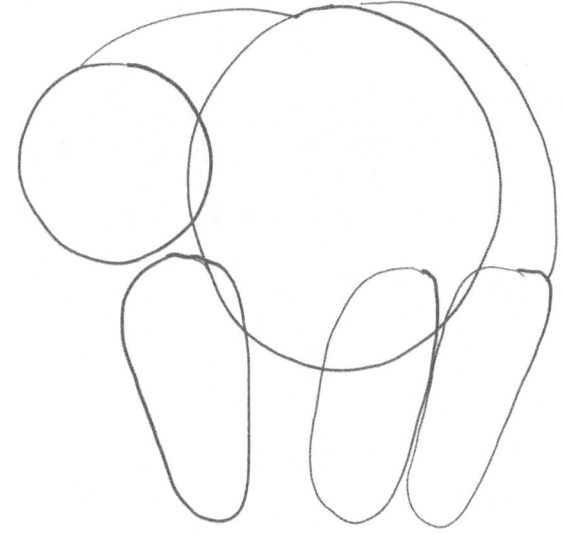

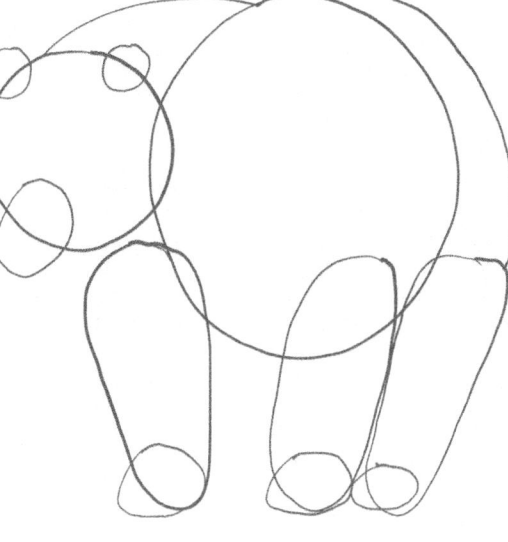

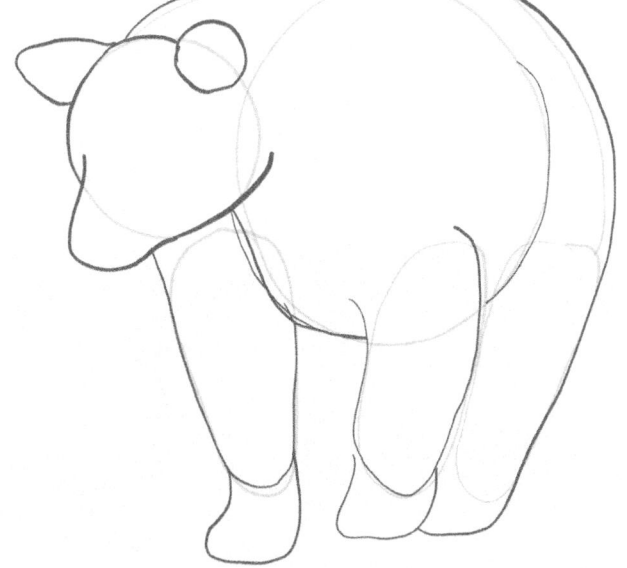

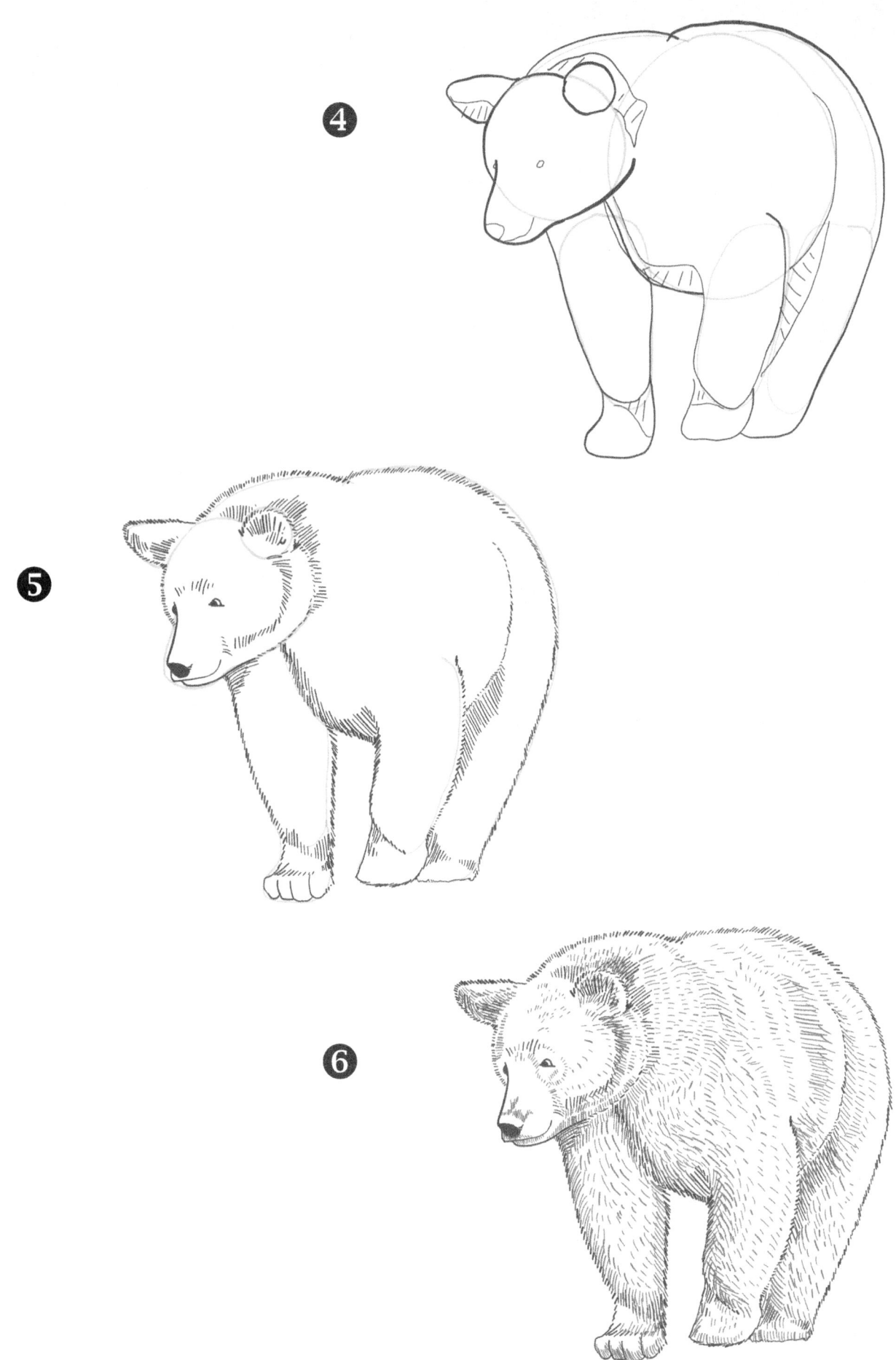

PRACTICE

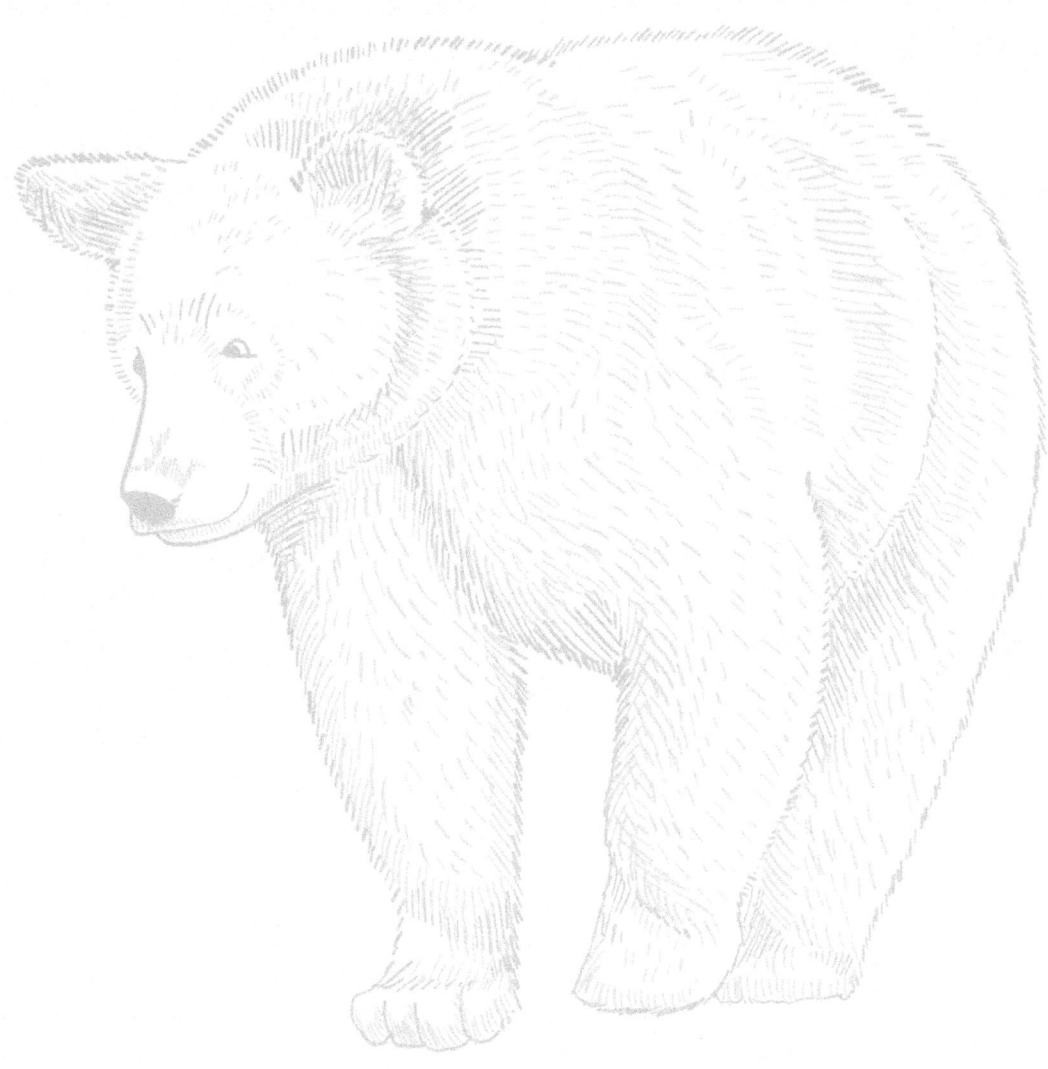

This page intentionally left blank as the back of the practice page

DRAWING A LION

 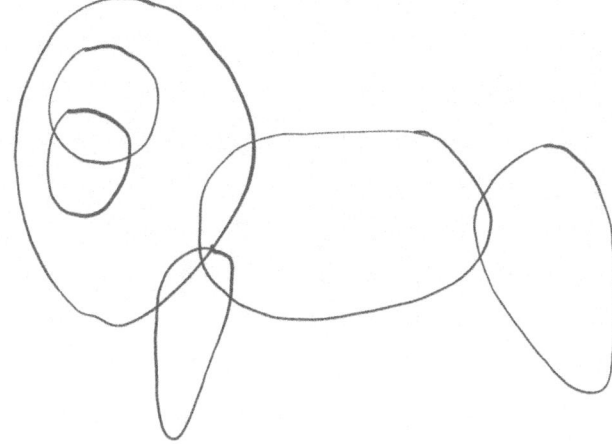

 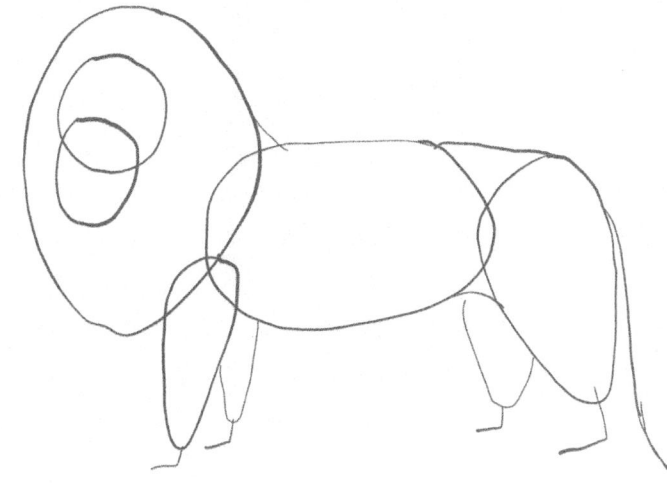

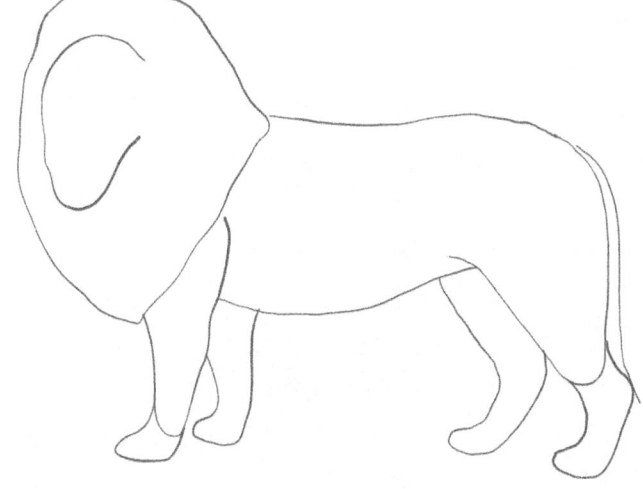

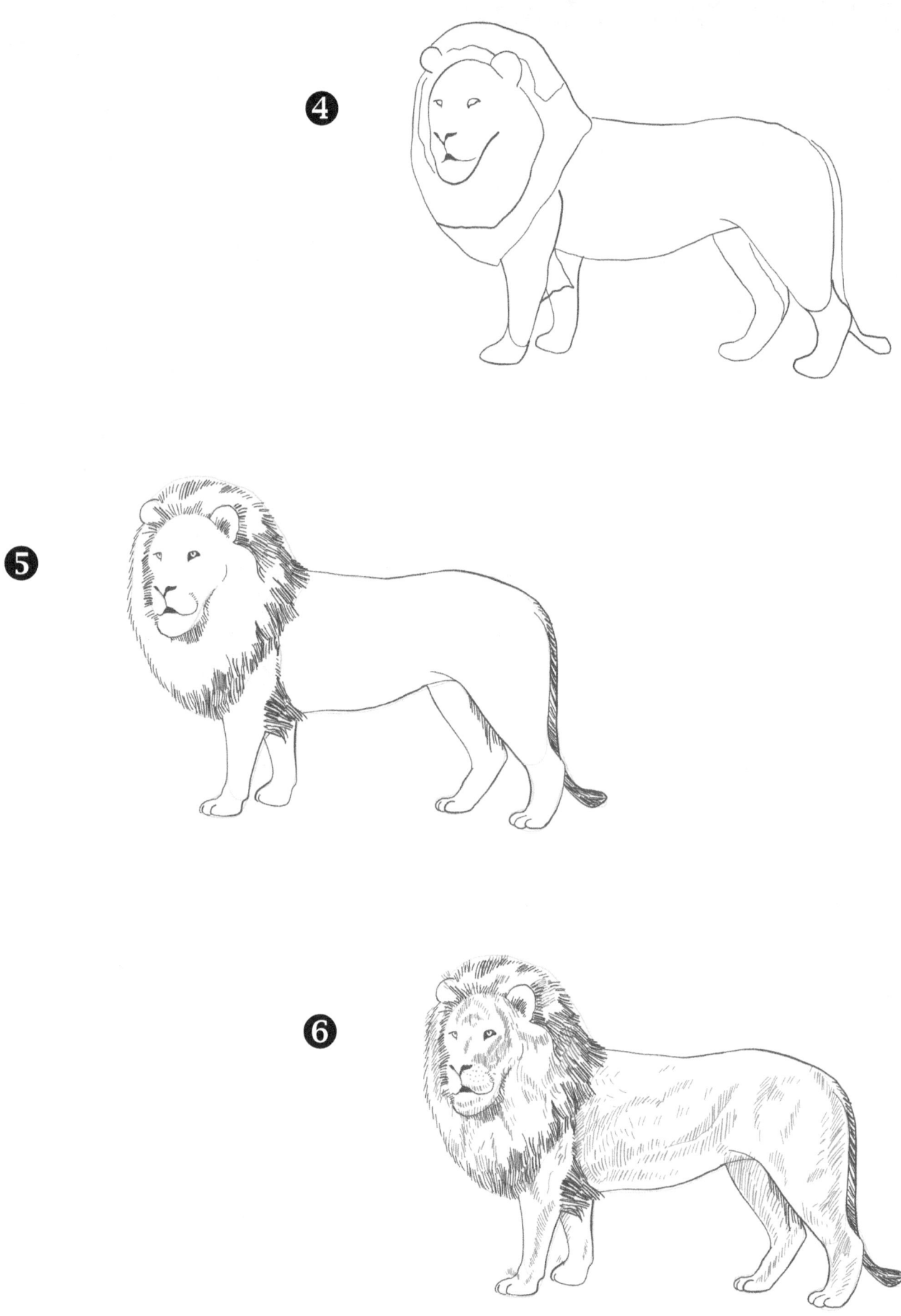

PRACTICE

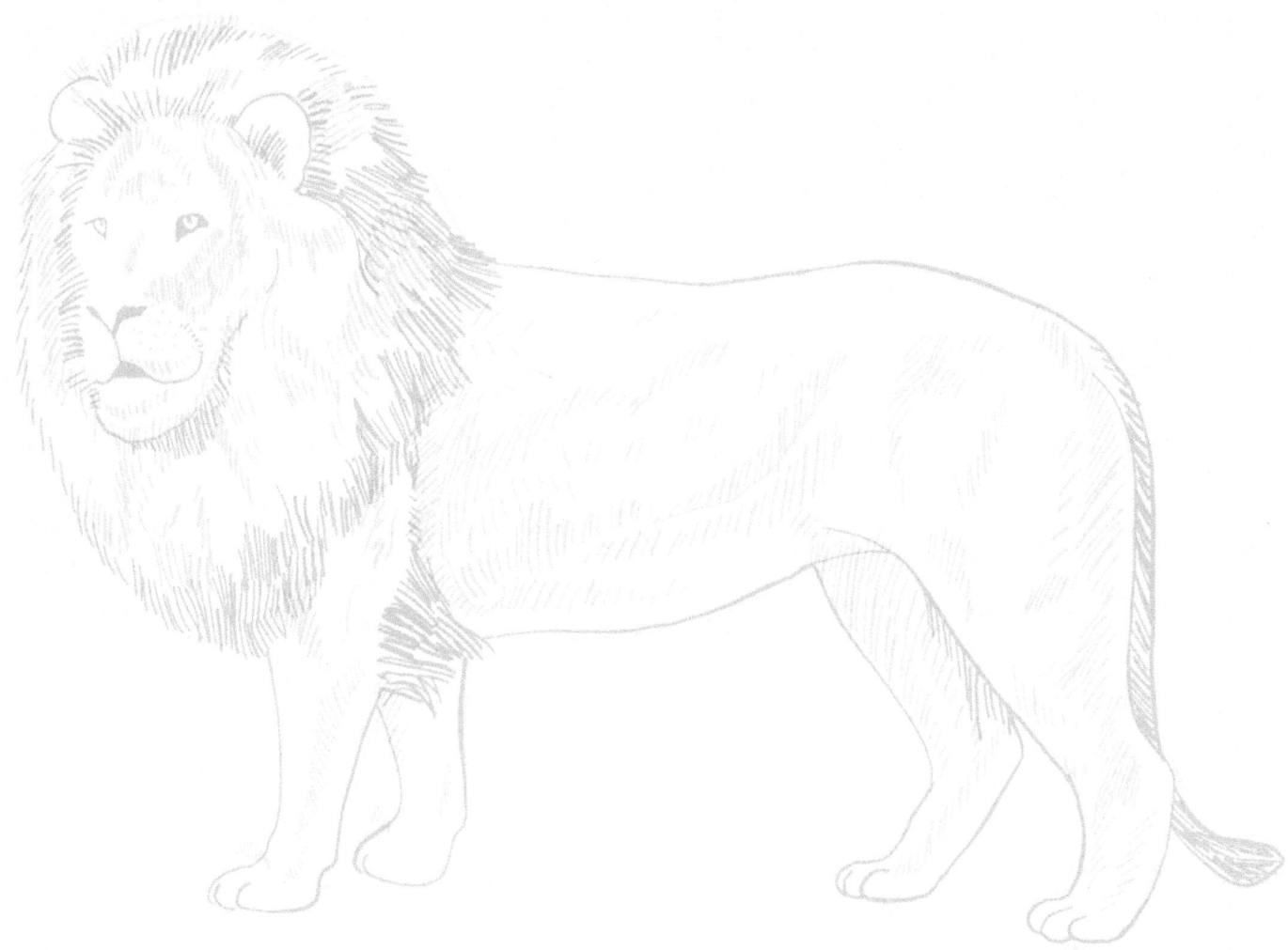

This page intentionally left blank as the back of the practice page

DRAWING A COW

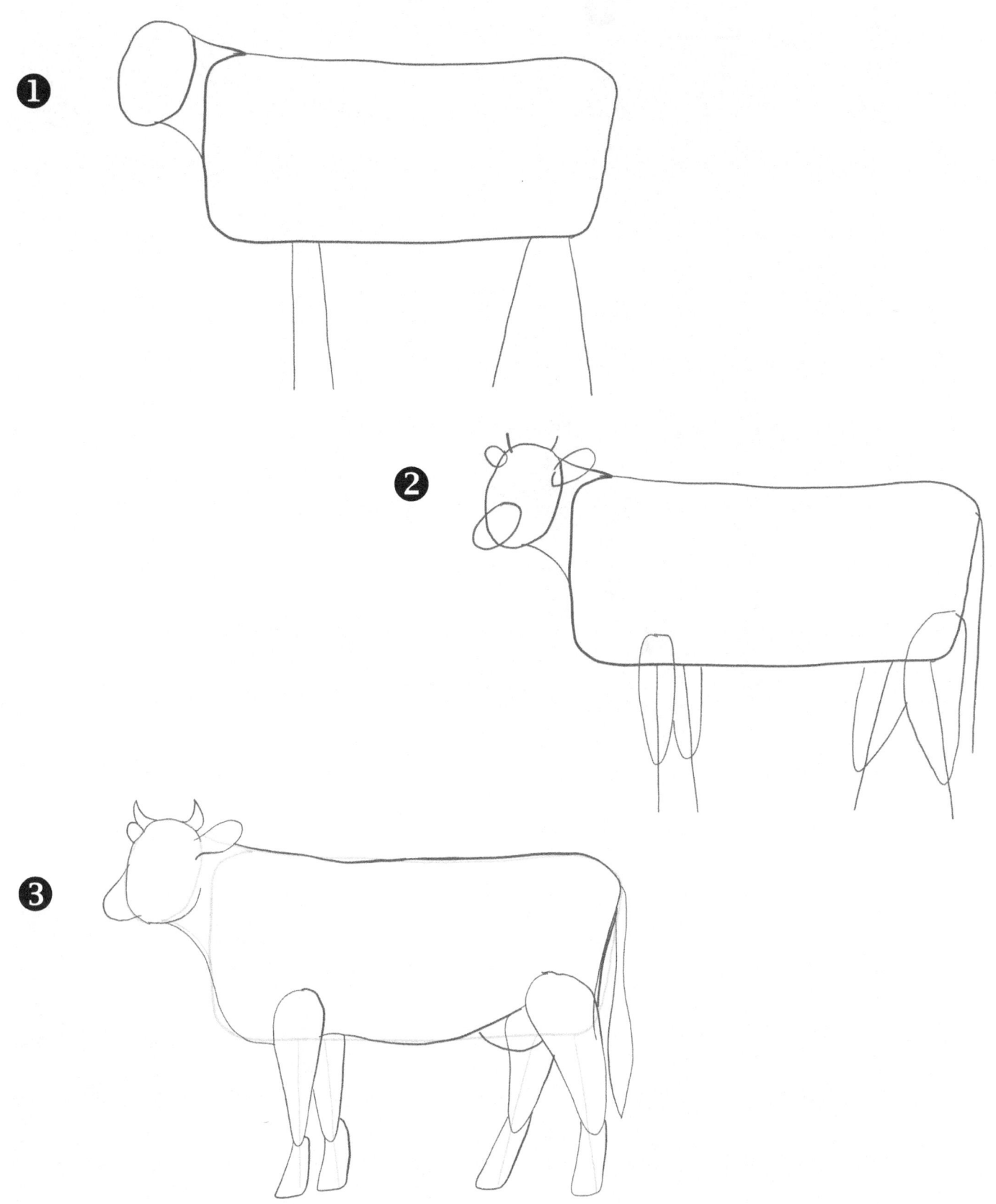

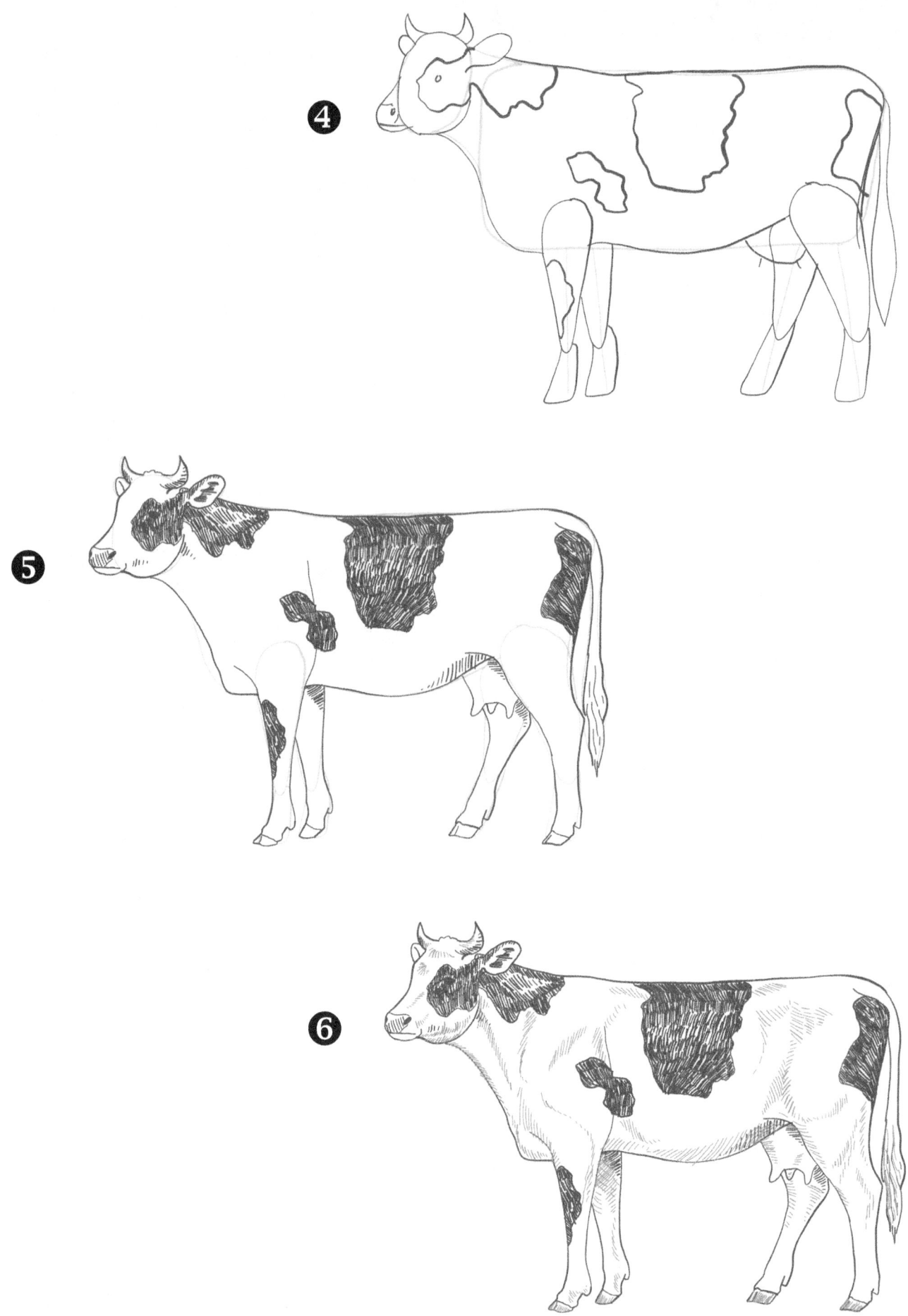

PRACTICE

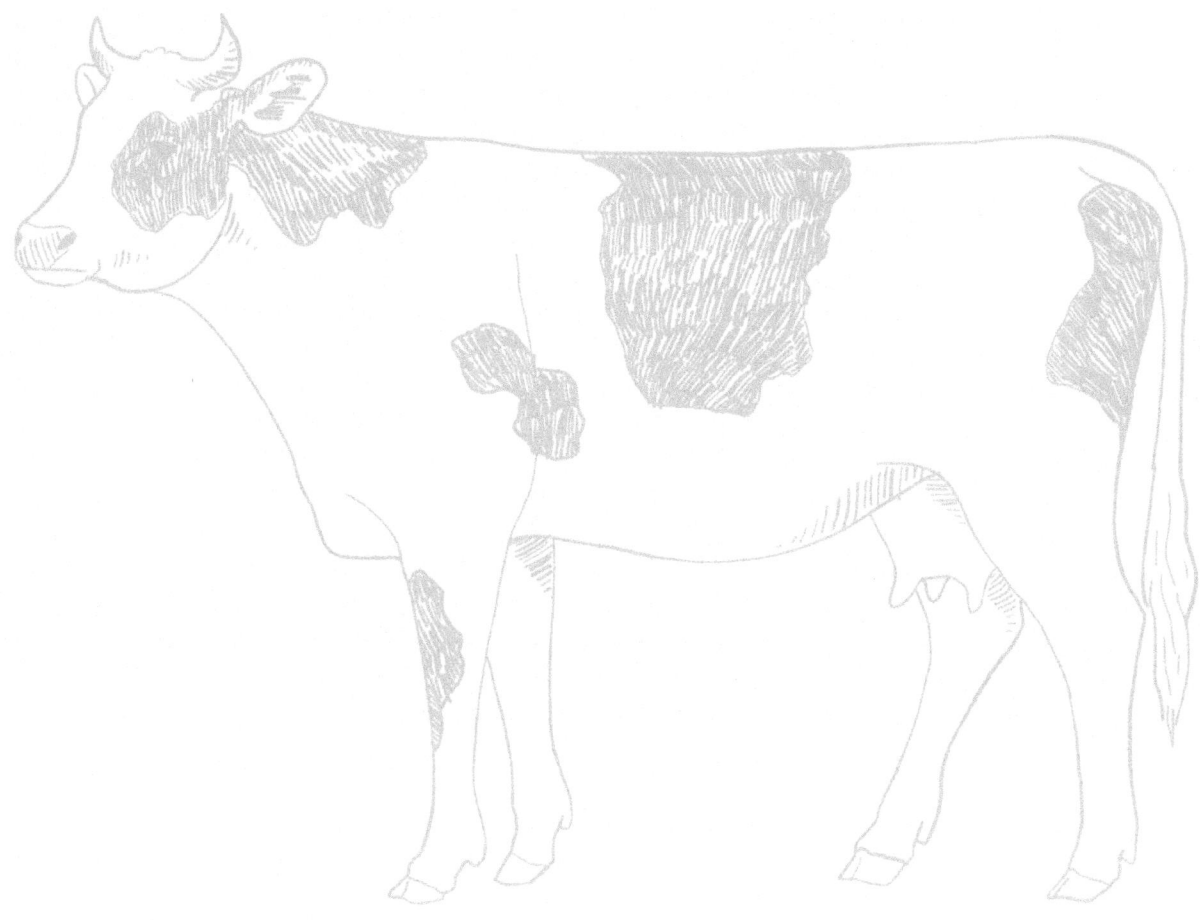

This page intentionally left blank as the back of the practice page

DRAWING A GIRAFFE

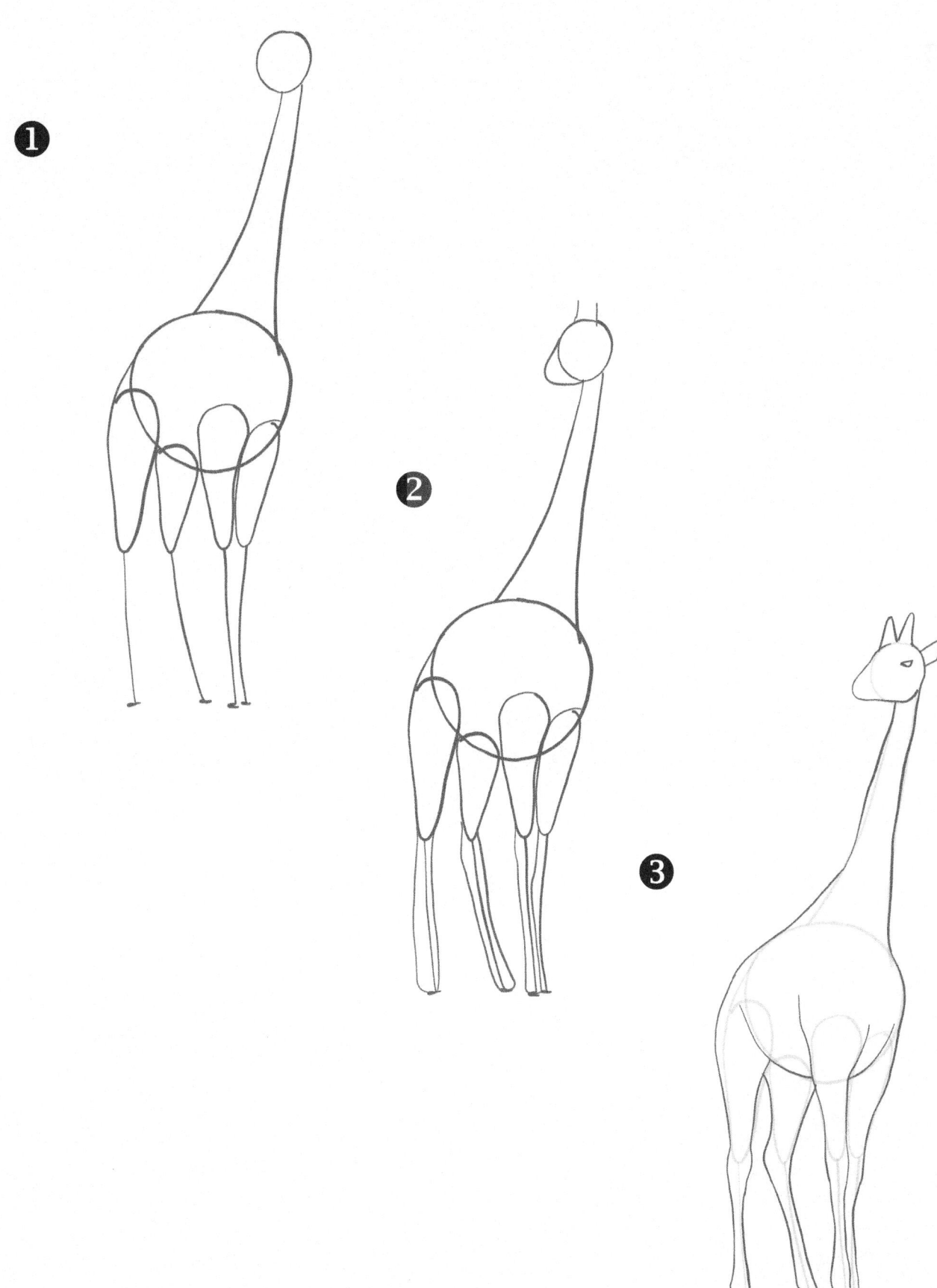

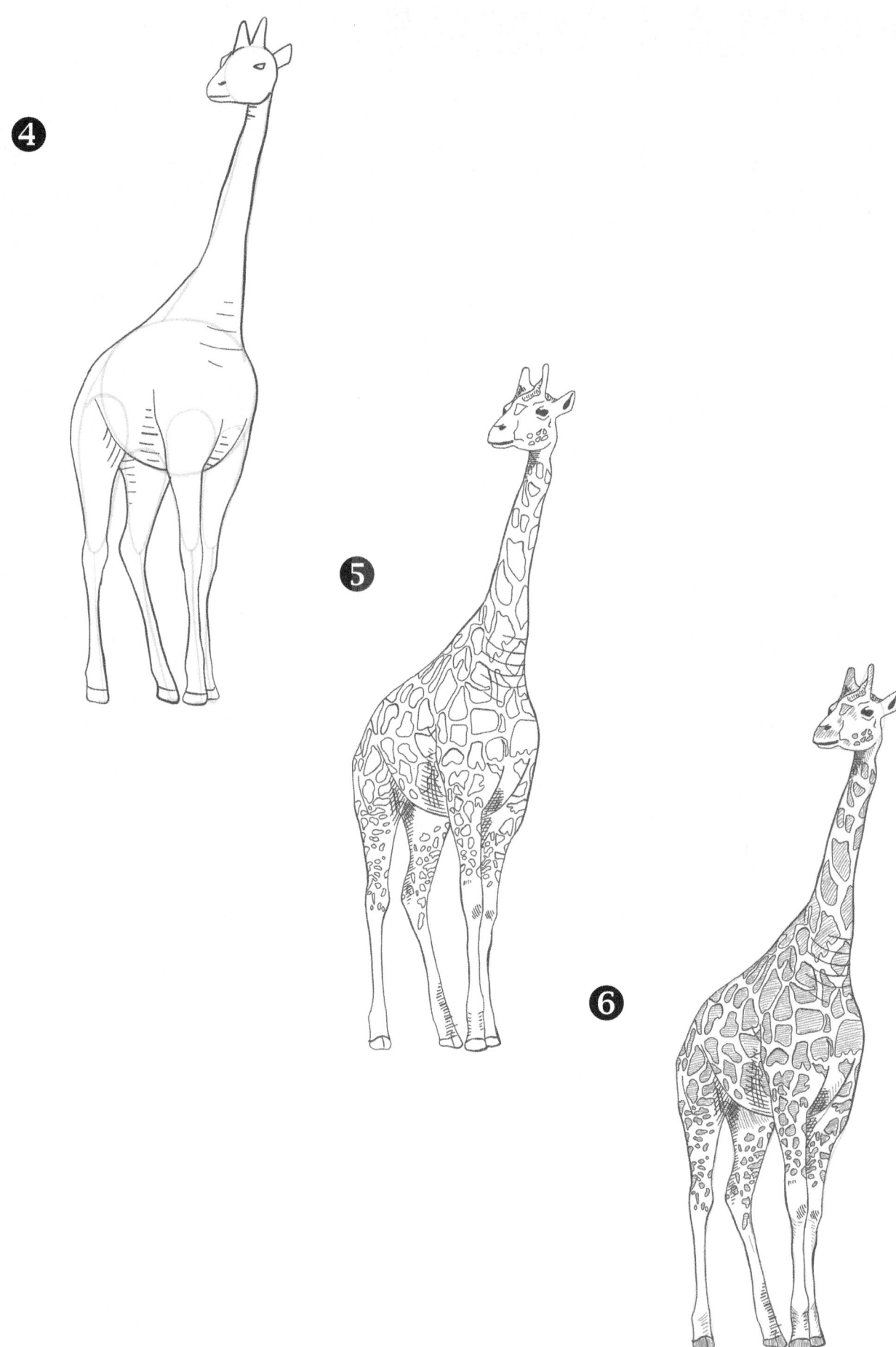

PRACTICE

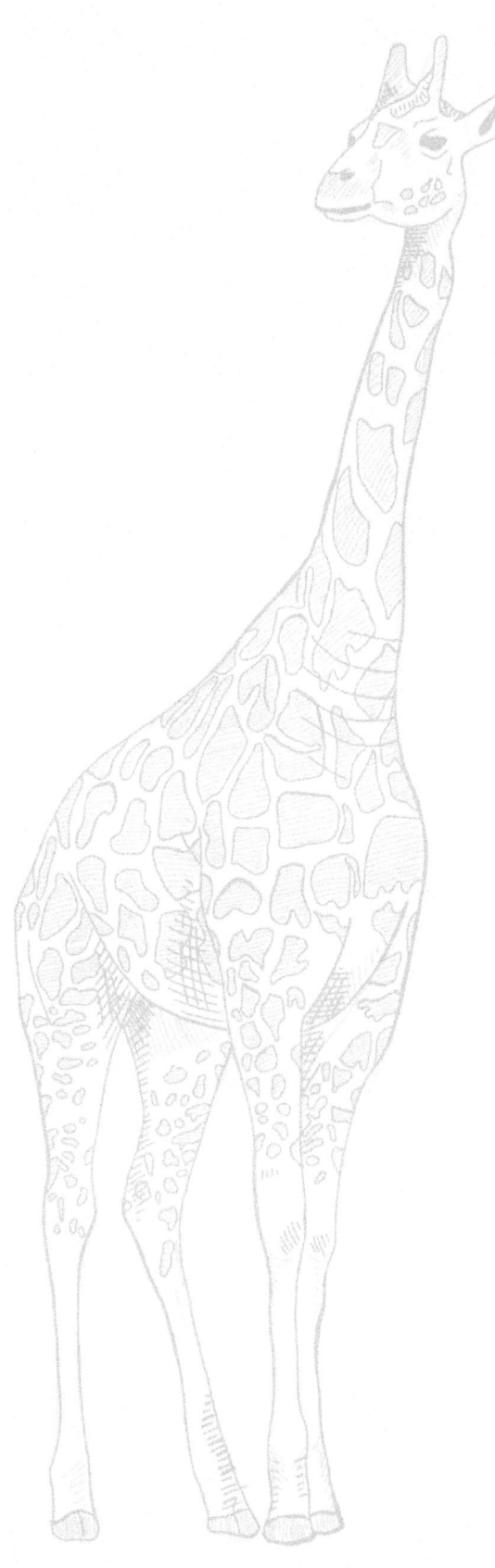

This page intentionally left blank as the back of the practice page

DRAWING A HORSE

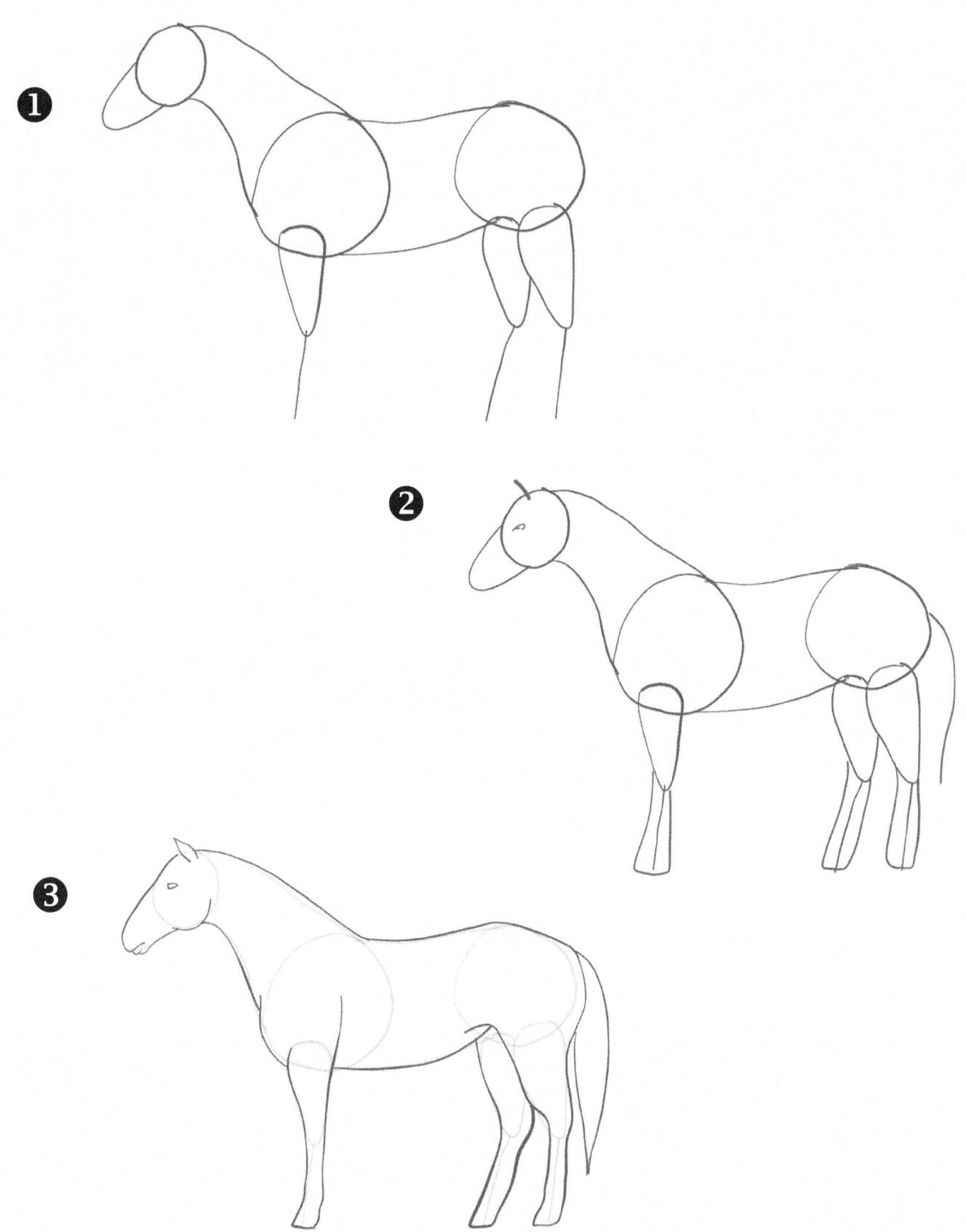

DRAWING A HORSE

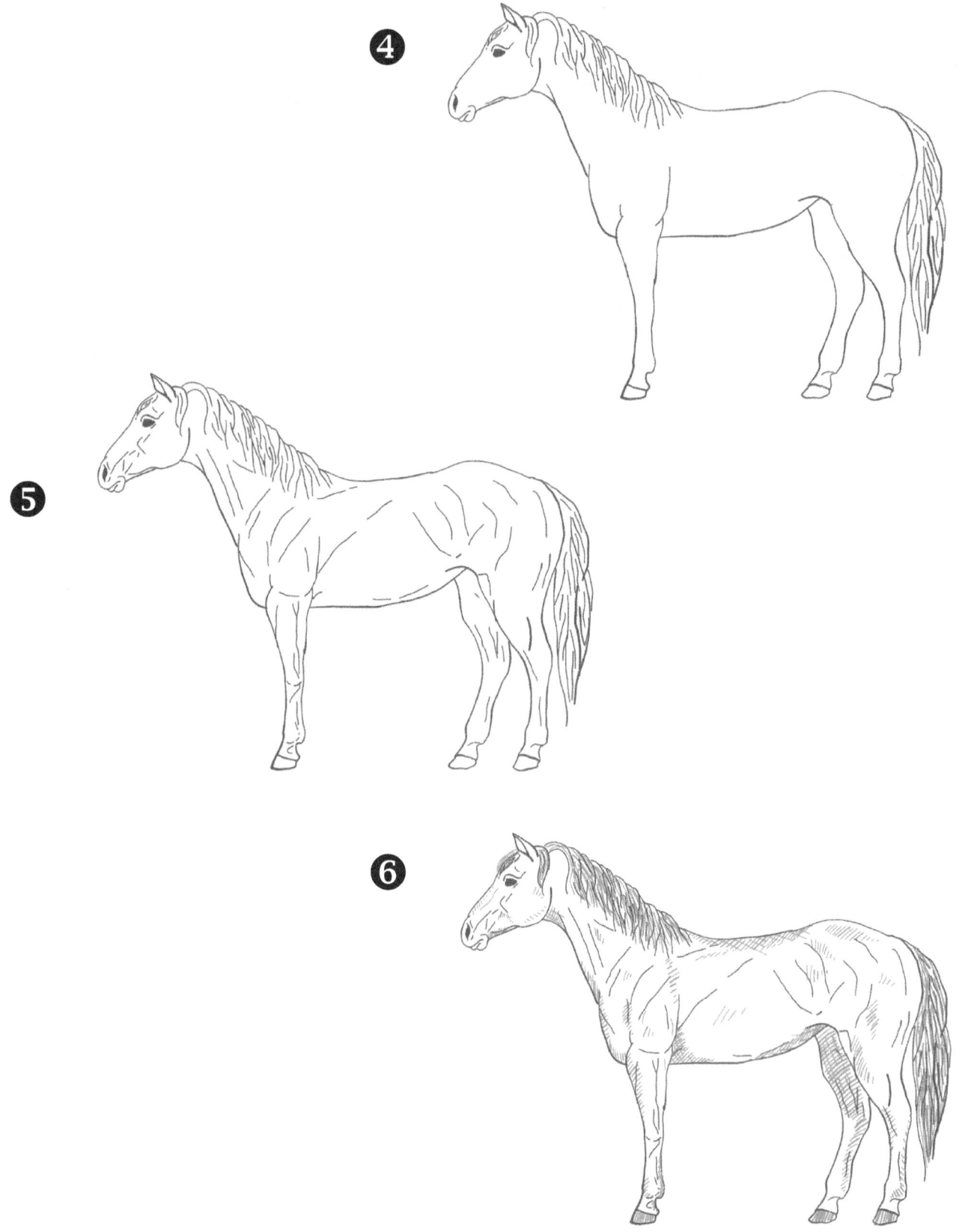

PRACTICE

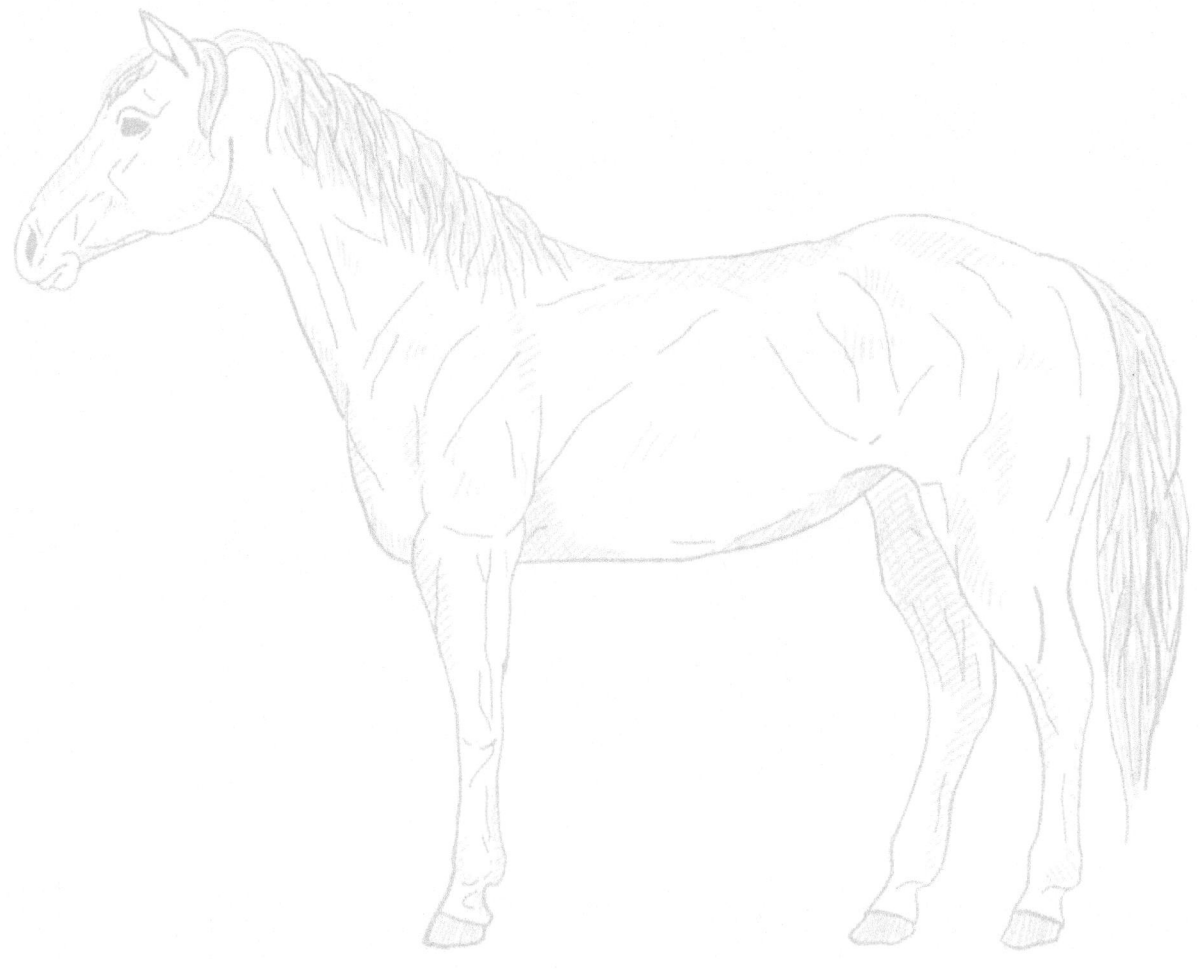

This page intentionally left blank as the back of the practice page

DRAWING AN OWL

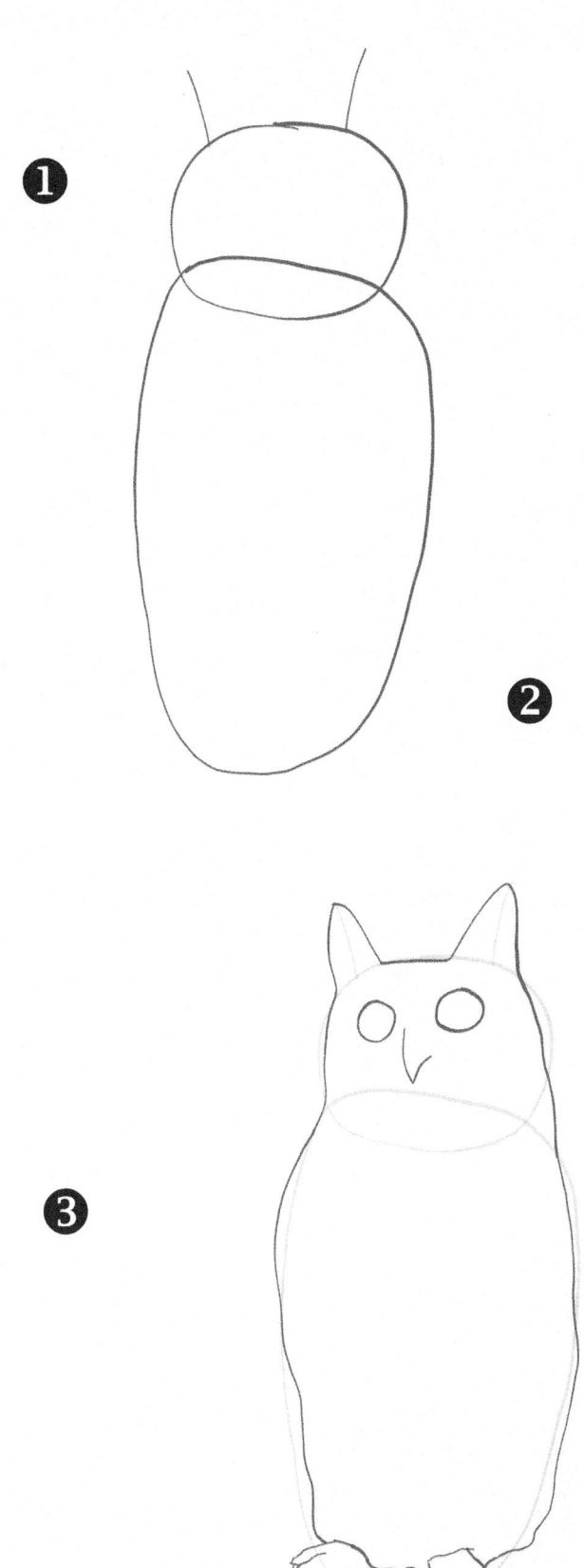

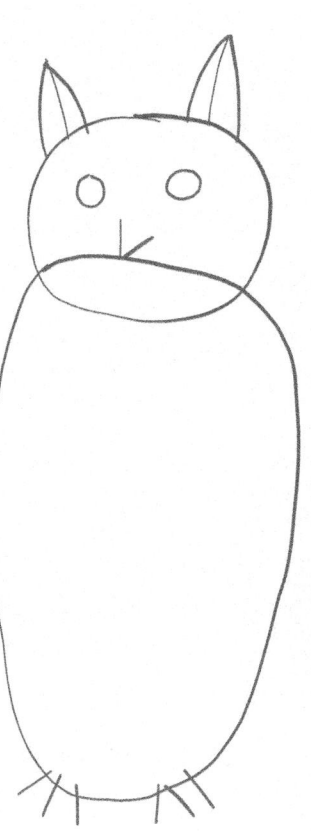

DRAWING AN OWL

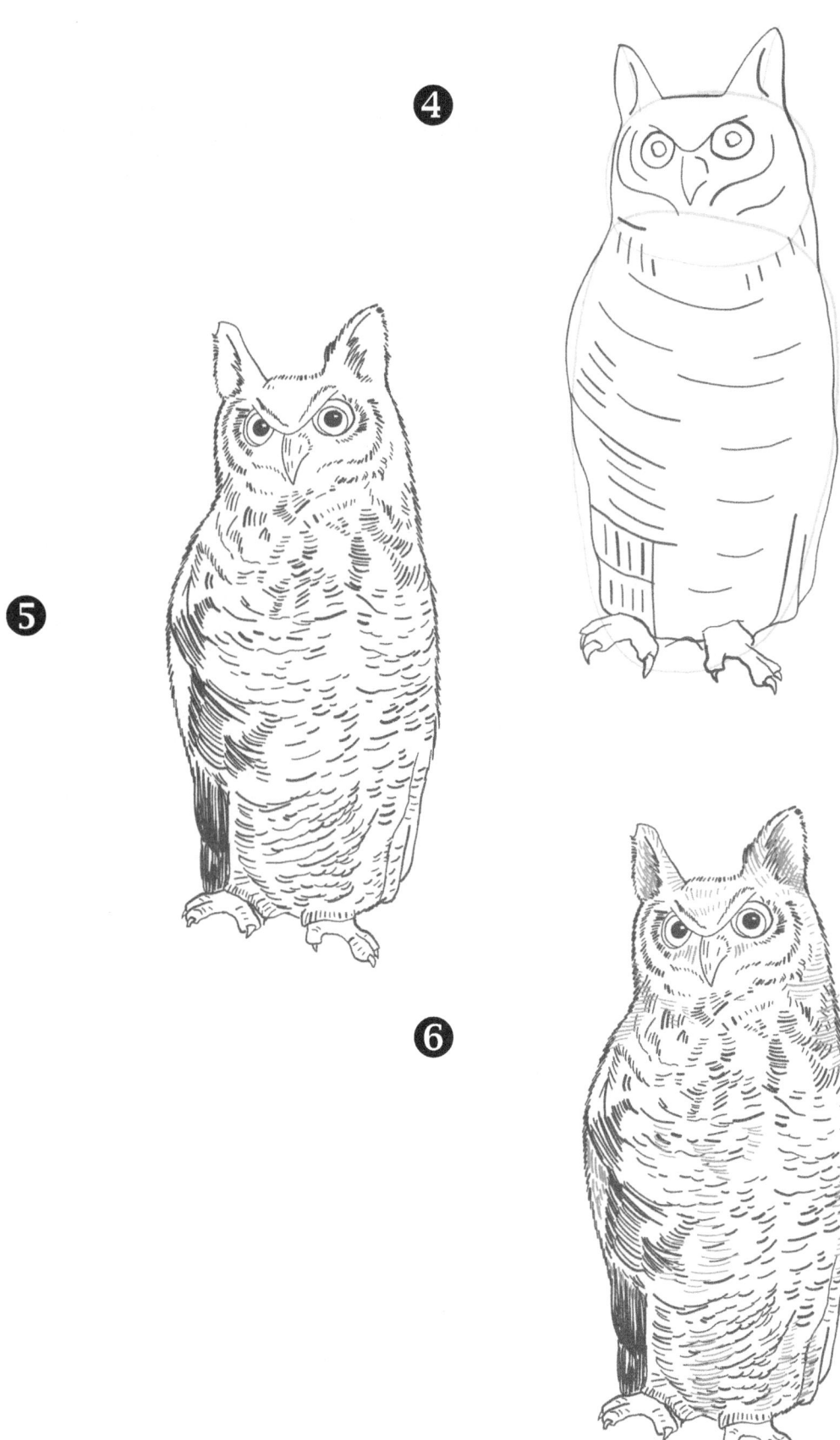

PRACTICE

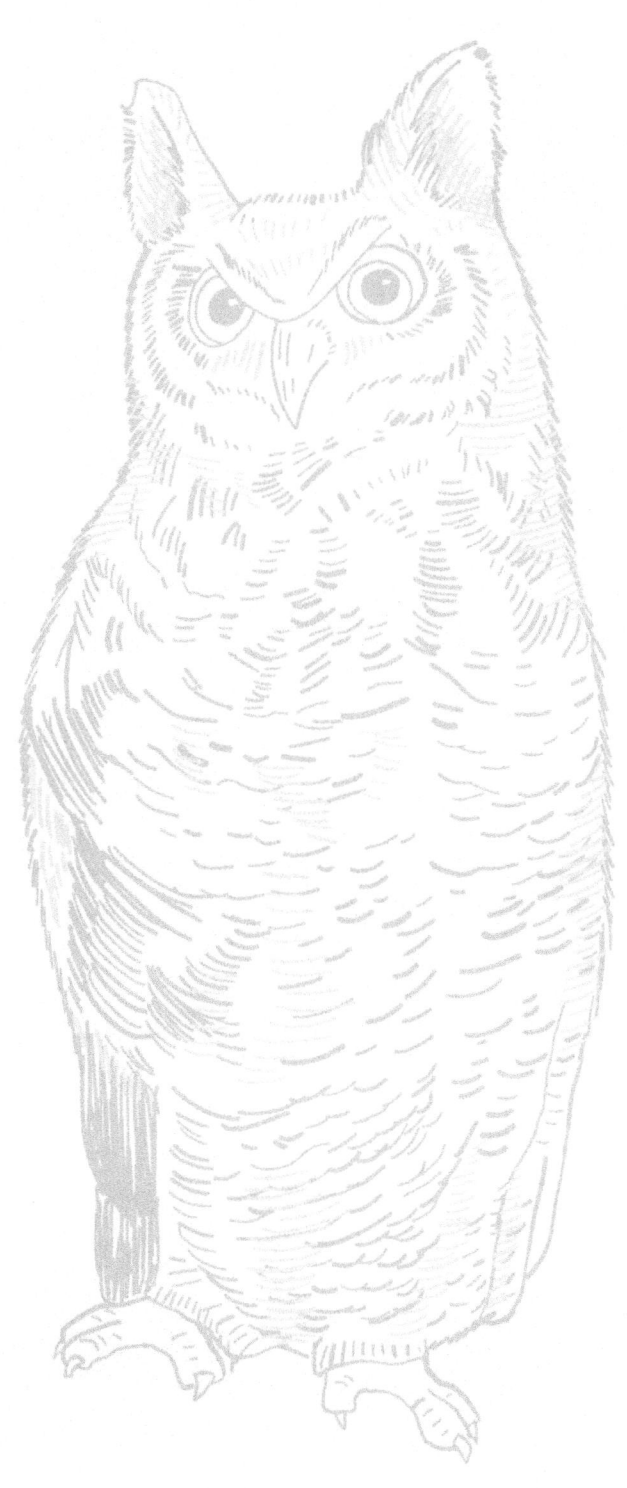

This page intentionally left blank as the back of the practice page

DRAWING A SQUIRREL

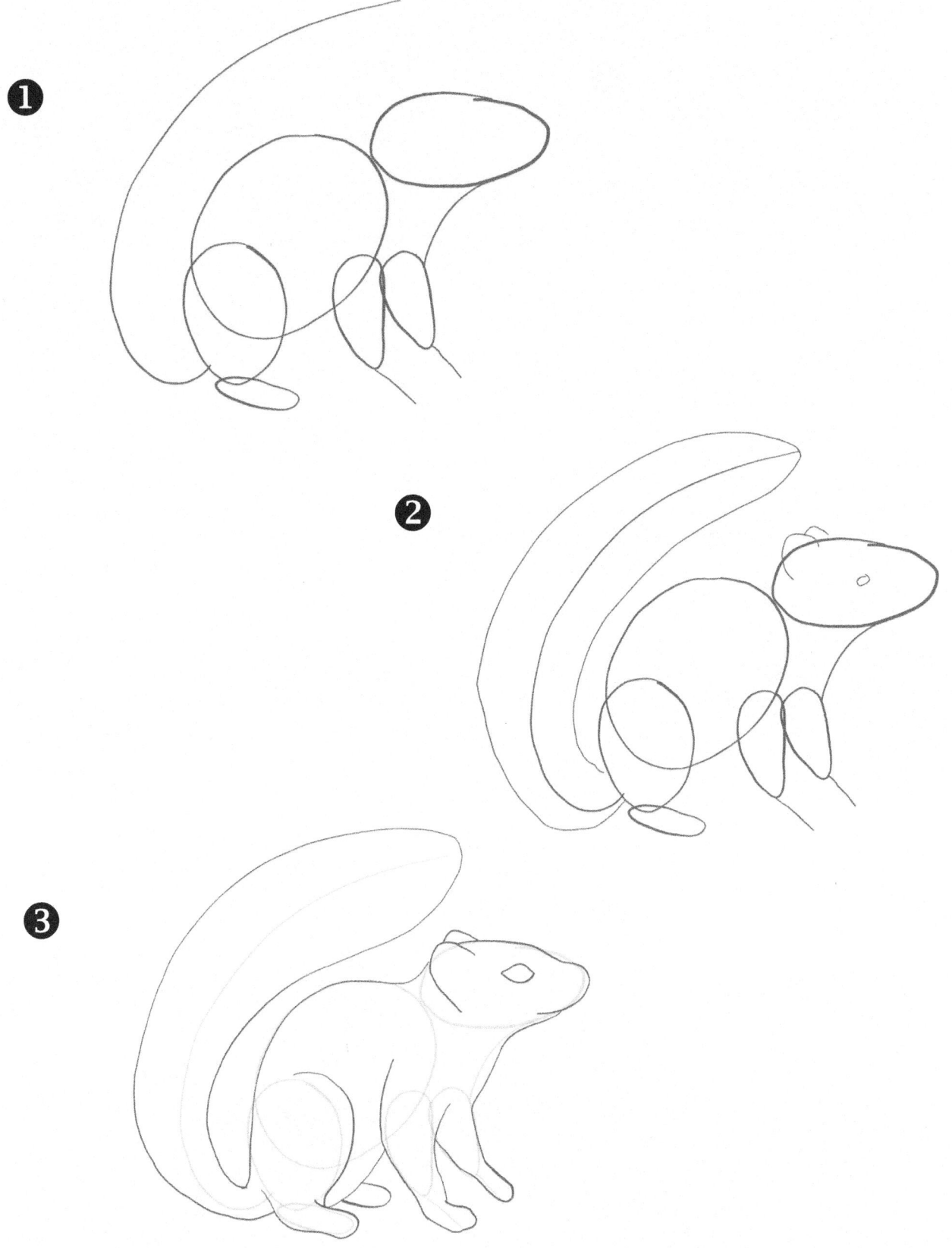

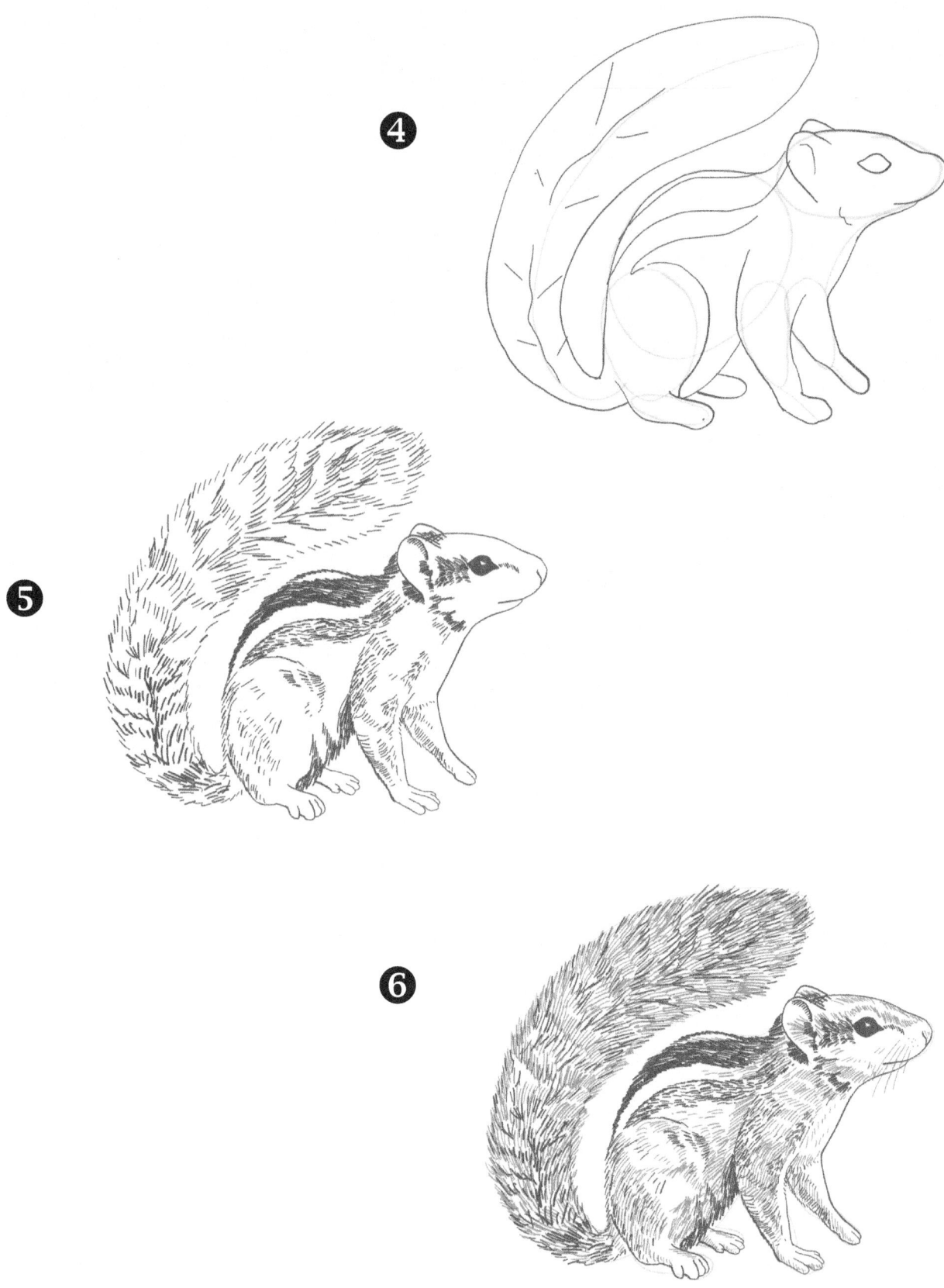

PRACTICE

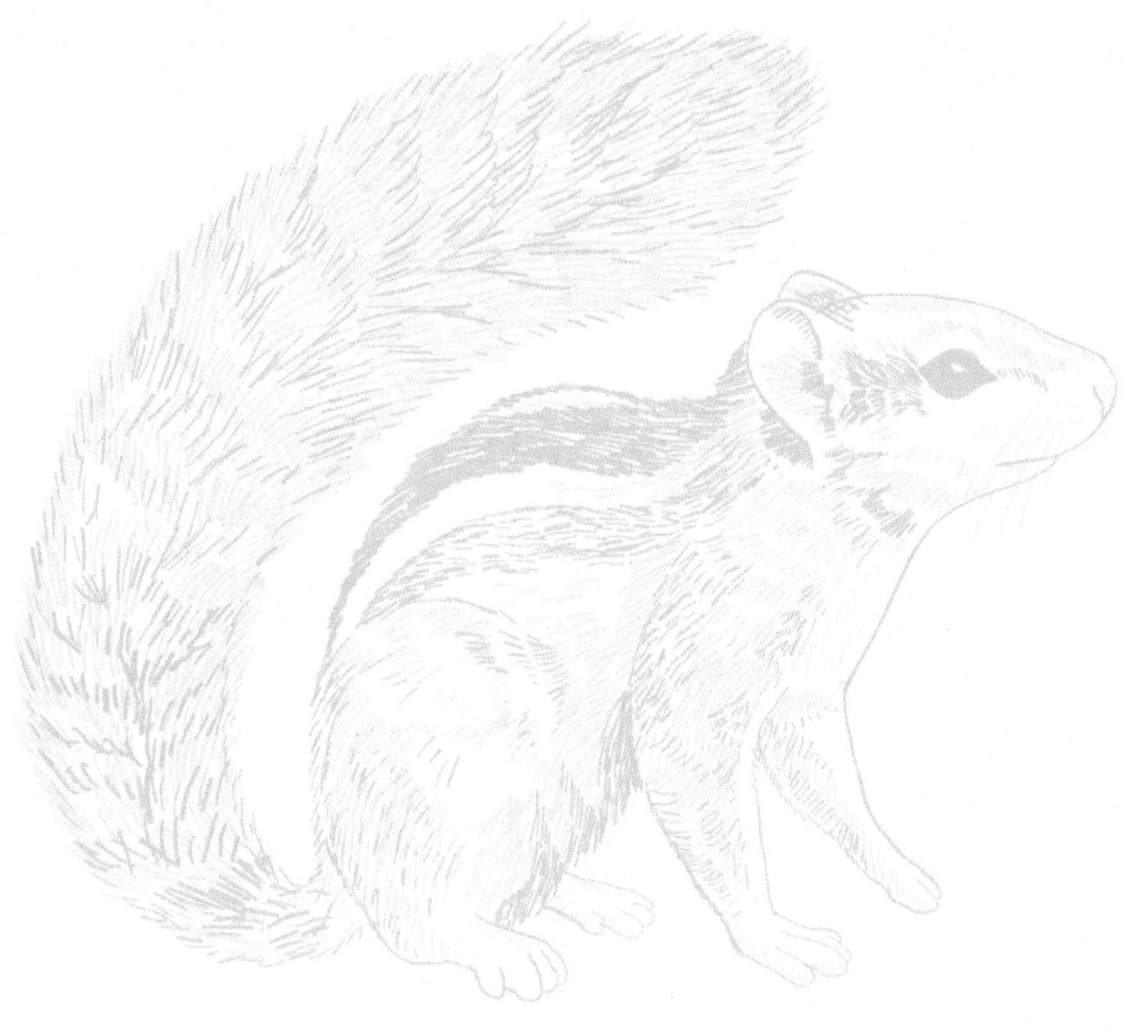

This page intentionally left blank as the back of the practice page

DRAWING A SEA TURTLE

①

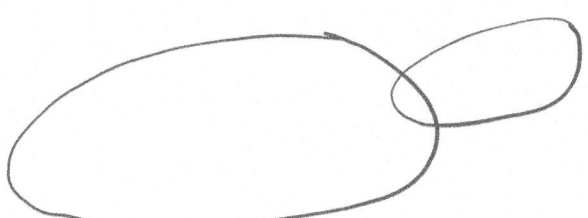

②

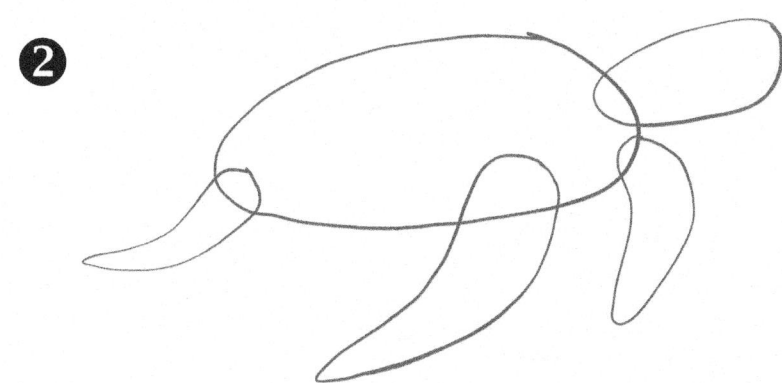

③

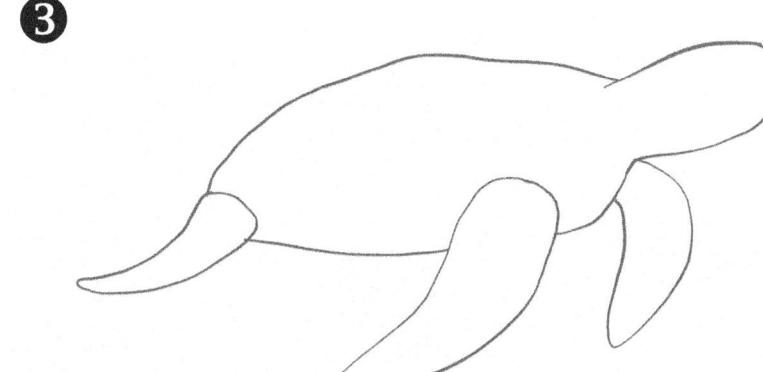

④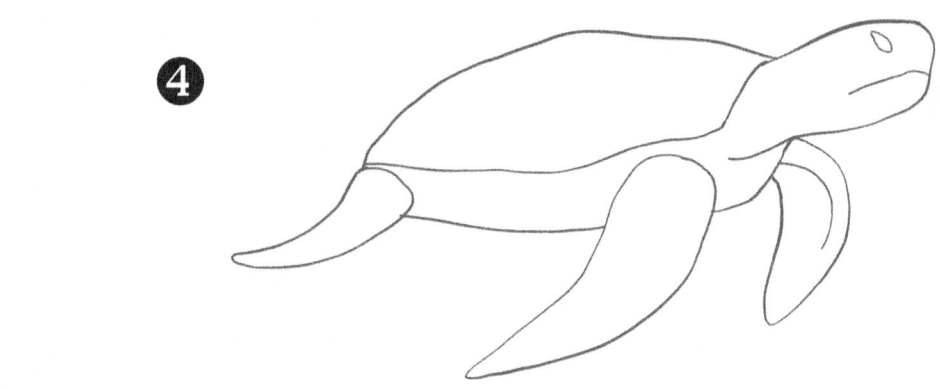

⑤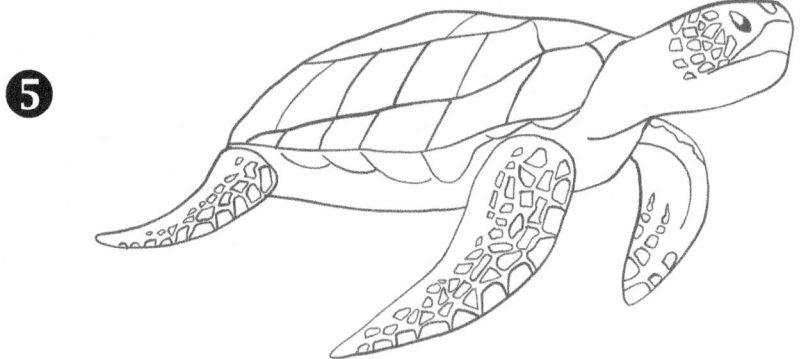

⑥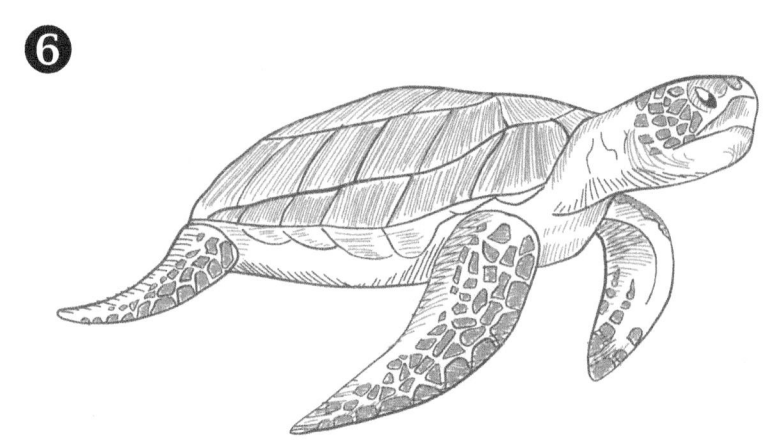

PRACTICE

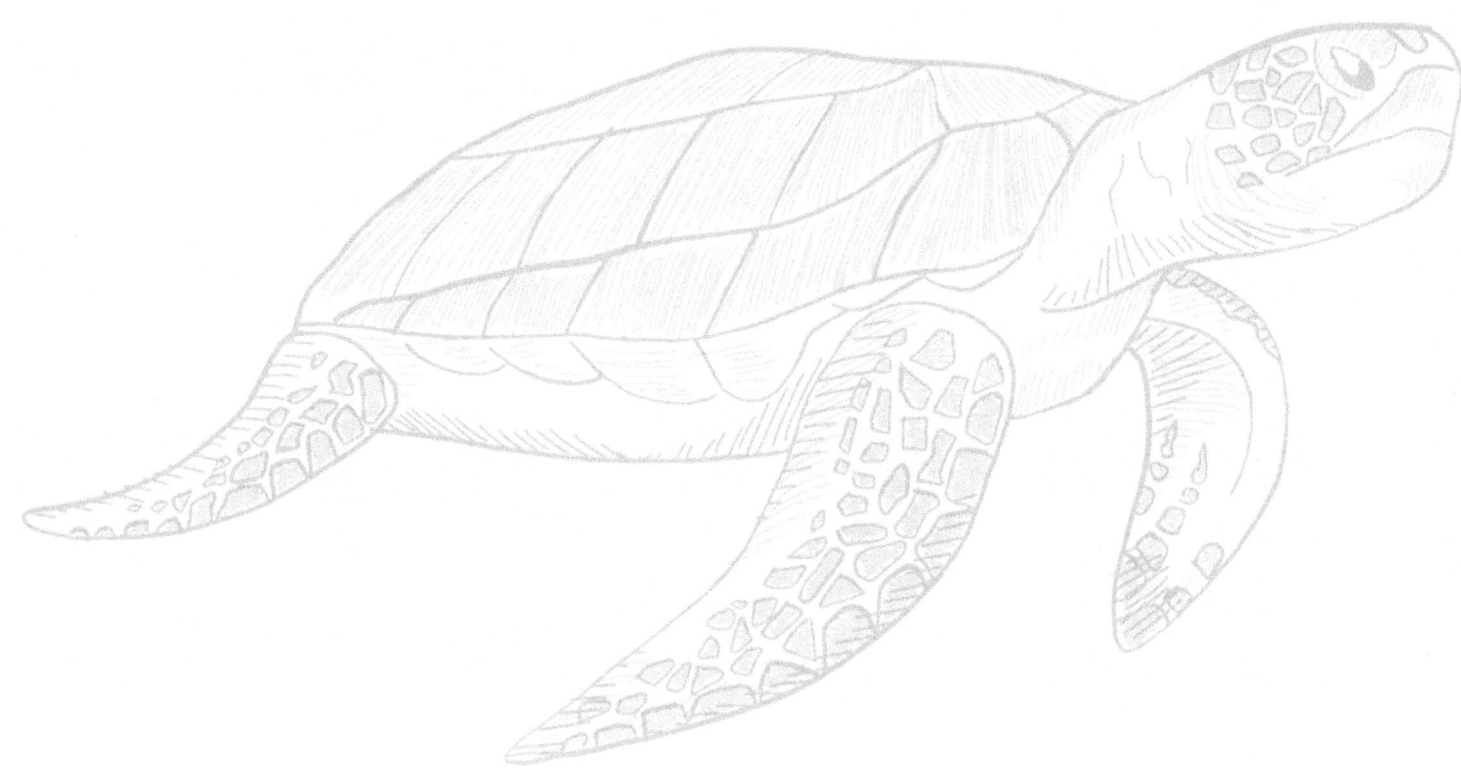

This page intentionally left blank as the back of the practice page

DRAWING AN ORCA WHALE

❶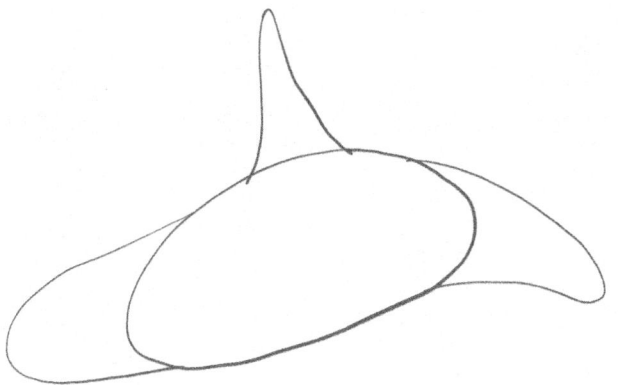

❷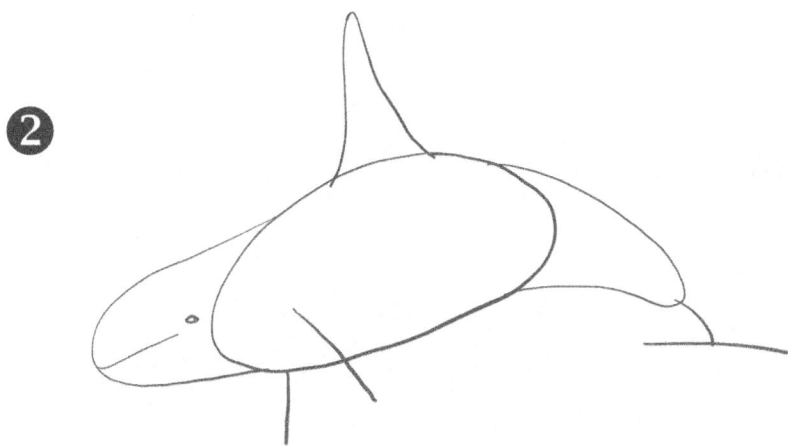

❸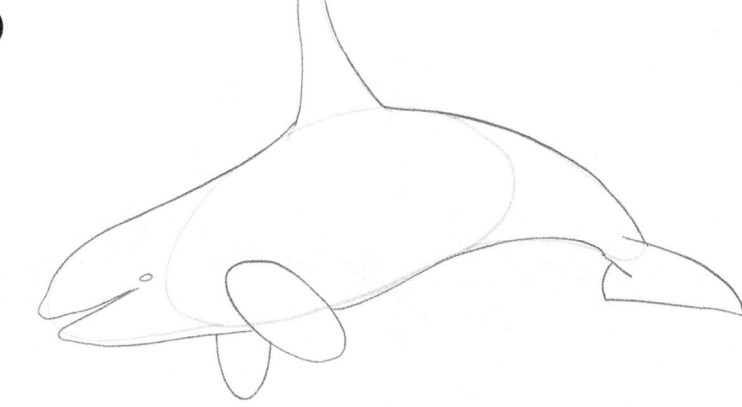

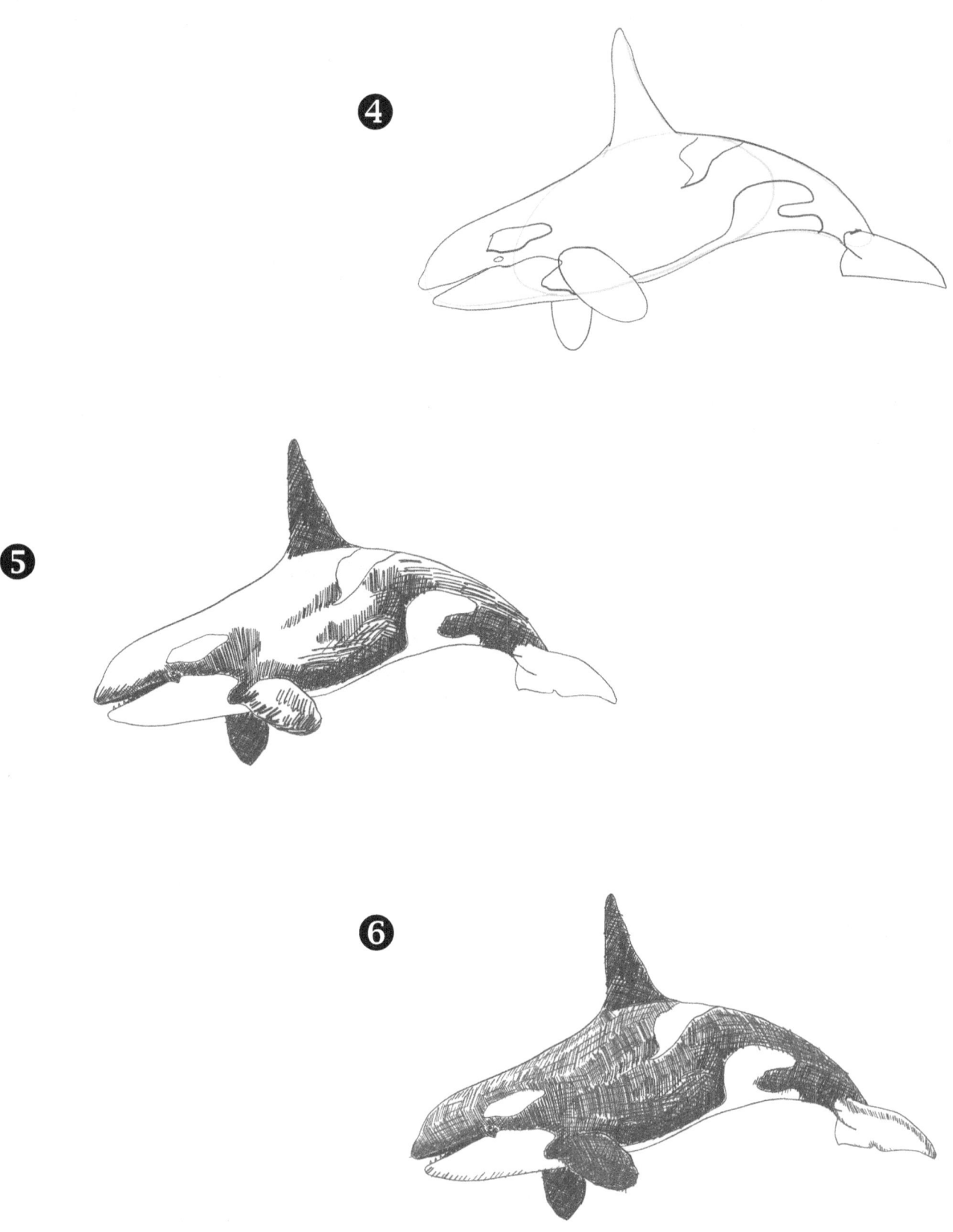

PRACTICE

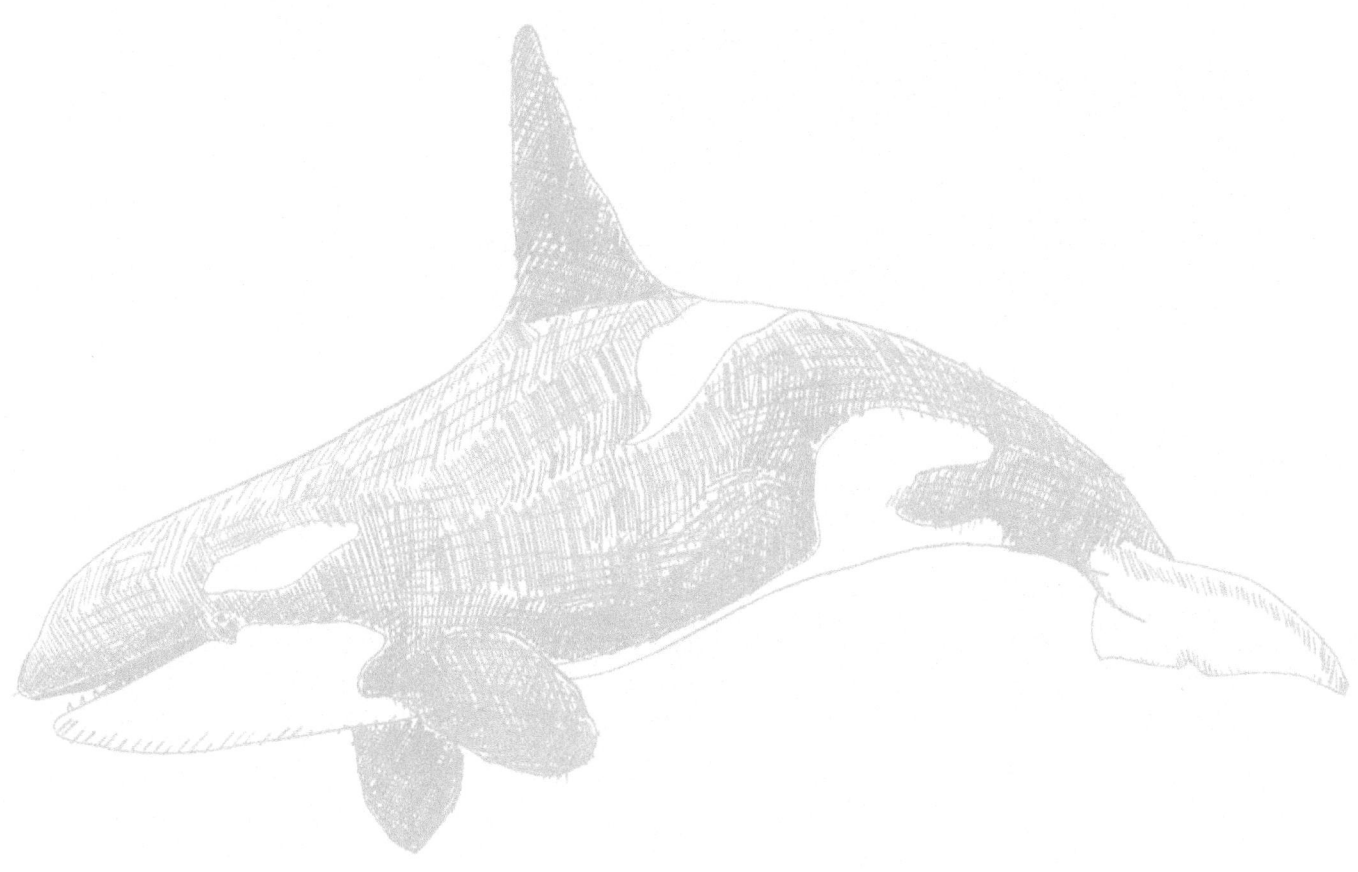

This page intentionally left blank as the back of the practice page